I0938556

STAGE ACTING
TECHNIQUES

STAGE ACTING
TECHNIQUES

John Hester

The Crowood Press

First published in 2004 by
The Crowood Press Ltd
Ramsbury, Marlborough
Wiltshire SN8 2HR

www.crowood.com

British Library Cataloguing-in-Publication Data
A catalogue record for this book is available from the British Library.

ISBN 1 86126 686 3

Typeset by NBS Publications, Basingstoke, Hampshire

Printed and bound in Great Britain by Biddles Ltd, King's Lynn.

CONTENTS

1 INTRODUCTION 9

2 THE 'REAL' ACTOR 11

3 THE ACTOR ALONE 21

4 ACTING WITH OTHERS 33

5 IMPROVISATION 45

6 MOVEMENT 53

7 VOICE 65

8 CHARACTERIZATION 77

9 FACING THE AUDIENCE 89

10 TAMING SHAKESPEARE 99

11 ACTING COMEDY 107

12 'THE PLAY'S THE THING' 115

FURTHER READING 125

INDEX 126

THE ACTING TECHNIQUES ENSEMBLE

Many thanks to the following actors for appearing in the photographs in this book:

Laura Budd
Richard Cole
Andrew Cottingham
Helen Dixon
Simon Holland
Ben Lewis
Adrian Lloyd James
Ken Lodge

Liz Meason
Francesca Peschier
Leah Tansey
Suzanne Taylor

Cover pictures:
(FRONT) Michael Gambon and Daniel Craig in the production *A Number* at the Royal Court Theatre, September 2002. Photo: Robbie Jack (BACK) Hugo Speer and Jannie Dee in the production *Betrayal* at the Duchess Theatre, London, February 2003. Photo: Robbie Jack

DEDICATION

For my parents.

ACKNOWLEDGEMENTS

This book is a product of my experience as a theatre professional over many years, and my own modest interpretation of a Stanislavski-based approach to acting. As such, although it represents my views and methods, it is inevitably influenced and enriched by the tuition that I myself have benefited from and the expertise of others I have absorbed. I would like to acknowledge particularly the Webber Douglas Academy of Dramatic Art (where I received a superb training), the director, David Wylde (who gave me the best of starts in the profession) and my tutor Hilary Wood, who, in my opinion, is the finest of acting techers. Without their wisdom and discipline I could not have worked in the theatre or written this book.

1 INTRODUCTION

HOW TO USE THIS BOOK

It is assumed that, as you have decided to read this book, you are either a practising actor who is wise enough to want to develop your skills, or someone who is considering acting for the first time and who wishes to have a fundamental grasp of the techniques involved from the outset. It is also possible that you are a teacher of drama looking for new ideas or a concrete system upon which to base your teaching. Whatever your motivation for coming to these pages, there is much within the book for you.

Acting is a craft and, as such, it not only requires natural talent, but a knowledge and understanding of the techniques and skills needed to apply it. Certainly, each reader of this book will, at this time, possess different levels of talent and experience. However, this does not matter, for the contents herein are designed to benefit all, at whatever stage of development they may be: the study of acting technique enables and empowers the student to make the most of their gifts and constantly improve upon their abilities.

It is also of no consequence whether you are approaching this work as an amateur or professional. While it is usually taken for granted that the professional will be constantly searching for, and experimenting with, new ideas and ways to develop as an actor, it is often the case that the amateur actor fails to see the necessity for this. This is a great shame, as there is absolutely no reason why every actor who practises their craft with love, whether it is their career or hobby, should not wish to be as good as they possibly can. Many other activities include the continual taking of lessons and instruction as an accepted requirement (sports, for instance), but when it comes to acting, there can be a misconception that talent and desire are enough, and that a practical attitude towards development is not necessary. This could not be further from the truth. Therefore, whoever you are, you are to be congratulated for coming to this book with an open mind and a desire to learn.

As you will discover, one of the main tenets of the book is that acting is a subject that has, by its very nature, to be practised mainly in groups, the members of which all need to be equally committed to developing their craft. However, it must also be acknowledged that you will, of course, be reading this book alone and therefore the instruction has been designed with that in mind. An emphasis has been placed on providing you with information that can be digested as you read, so that its wisdom may then be practised whenever you act, both in rehearsal and performance. Many of the exercises are designed for one person alone and these may be experimented with as and when you are ready. It is hoped that the exercises that require two or more participants will inspire you to

OPPOSITE: **Trust and clear communication are both vital for actors.**

practise them with friends and colleagues, either immediately or after you have finished reading the book. However, if this is not possible, simply reading and analysing them will still benefit you greatly and enrich your understanding of acting. For these reasons, the exercises have not been separated and reside within the text as a whole.

You will be able to be as proactive about working with this book as you wish to be. You may simply want to read it through quietly in your chair and absorb its instruction for a later day, and it will certainly work for you in this way. At the other end of the scale, you may wish to use the book as the basis for a course or series of workshops for your group, company or society, tackling each subject matter sequentially and completing the exercises in full – this too will work extremely well. However you approach the content of these pages, ensure that you do so with commitment and energy, and have confidence that you are capable of improving your skills immeasurably.

Also remember that a book of this nature, while comprehensive, must always be viewed as a starting point. It is hoped that you will not only be inspired to go out and put into effect what you have learnt, but become hungry to discover and learn more too.

STARTING OUT

Before you start upon your journey, you must consider some important points regarding the manner in which you should conduct your studies.

If you are working alone, it is vital that you use your imagination to illustrate the various techniques and exercises in your mind. When reading about an exercise, whether you intend to practise it immediately or not, try to picture the scenario clearly in your head and envisage the various outcomes of its experimentation. Let the text of the book lead you towards its conclusions, so that you may share in them and be able to put them into practice when required.

When you decide to work upon any of the exercises, make sure you do so in a relaxed manner, with plenty of time at your disposal to complete them properly and in an environment that will allow you to focus fully upon implementing the instructions. Also ensure that you are wearing loose, comfortable clothing and appropriate footwear.

When you are working with others it is important that you do so in harmony and not competitively: you must have total trust in your colleagues in order to function without inhibition. To achieve this, take time to warm up and play some simple games before you start working properly. You can use a few of the movement and voice exercises that you will find in later chapters, and silly party games make excellent 'ice breakers' – freeing the imagination and building trust and respect.

Finally, make sure that your approach to the work is brave and bold. It is far better to give 100 per cent and fail, than it is to be cautious and timid and never realize your full potential. Feel that getting things wrong is absolutely permissible. It is only by allowing yourself, and others, to take risks that you will learn anything at all and ultimately become a good and proper actor. With this firmly in mind, start forth with confidence – and enjoy!

The 'Real' Actor

Grass Roots

When acting is stripped down to its basics – when the outer covering of complexity is ripped away and the very 'bottom line' of acting can be looked full in the face – something emerges that is really quite straightforward, simple and easy. Forget, for the moment, the various diversions of characterization and emotion – these exotic ingredients may remain on a theatrical 'back-burner' while you examine the essential ingredients of the recipe. The actor must not try to run before she or he can walk.

When a child learns to walk it stumbles, wobbles and falls, but, having mastered the skill of walking, begins to walk instinctively and takes its new-found skill for granted. So it must be with acting. Once the actor can metaphorically 'walk', without thinking about the process too deeply, running, skipping and even jumping will follow. Acting is indeed a great and complex craft, requiring immense skill and dedication, but its fundamentals are organic and, if you can grasp these fundamentals securely and properly, everything else will fall into place so much more easily. To begin with, you must ascertain an acceptable concept of what acting, in its basic and naked form, essentially is.

What is Acting?

Write down any and every definition of 'acting' that you can think of. In doing this, be personal – say what the word means to you and not what you think the right answer is. If you are in a group share your thoughts and try to develop the list. There are many possible responses. Here are just a few:

- being someone else
- using your imagination
- playing a role
- entertaining an audience
- bringing a play to life
- pretending something is real.

There is no right or wrong involved here. All of these are legitimate thoughts and indeed each person will see acting in a different way and with a different set of priorities. However, look again at your own list of definitions. As useful and pertinent as they may be as individual parts of the whole picture, you will still need an overall definition of the craft at its grass roots – a basic formula.

A Very Useful Definition

Examine the following definition: acting is the recreating of the natural processes of hearing, thinking and responding in the unnatural environment of knowing what you are going to hear, knowing what you are going to think and knowing how you are going to respond. This does not claim to be the only possible basic definition of 'acting', but it serves the purpose of a starting place. Of course, acting is many other things too: beautiful and exciting

things like exploring great and wonderful emotions; bringing fascinating and exotic characters to life; and stimulating the very souls of your audience. However, all of these things flow from a working understanding of this definition and you must now begin your journey towards that understanding. Repeat it to yourself and start to analyse what you think it might mean. As you unpick and dismantle it, as you come to understand it and apply its truth to your work, so you will discover an inbuilt ability to act better and more truthfully than you might expect.

In the Chair

This exercise requires 'a brave volunteer' who will perform the exercise, and a group of 'onlookers' who will observe and draw conclusions from the results of this particular experiment.

The volunteer sits in a chair and does nothing for exactly one minute. During this time the onlookers must watch him or her intently. If you are the volunteer do not try to define the meaning of 'nothing' before you start – it is important that you instinctively interpret what you think doing nothing is. If you are an onlooker you must keep your eyes on the volunteer throughout the sixty seconds. Actors must structure their work from the point of view of always being observed – for this is the very reason for acting and it must become a natural situation for the actor to experience.

When the minute is over the volunteer may relax and the onlookers take it in turns to state exactly what they observed during the time. This will vary but here are some of the usual comments:

OPPOSITE: **An actor's work must contain reality, commitment and truth.**

- 'He looked embarrassed.'
- 'She looked as if she was trying hard not to do anything.'
- 'His attention seemed to wander.'
- 'She looked as if she was about to laugh.'
- 'He looked tense and frozen to the chair.'
- 'She looked as if she didn't understand the exercise.'

The conclusion that can be drawn from all and any of these comments is that the volunteer was unable to obey the instructions of the exercise. They did not do 'nothing' as requested – they communicated. The communication may have been instinctive and may also have been misinterpreted by the onlookers, but 'communicate' they did and 'nothing' they did not. They must not be blamed for this, as they have illuminated the important truth that it is impossible to do nothing – for whatever else human beings may or may not do, they will always communicate in some way.

Instant Communication

By this simple exercise you have proved that whatever is in your head and heart (your thoughts and feelings) will communicate automatically through your body (and, of course, voice). In 'real life' you do not have to think about the mechanics of communicating. This is because the act of communicating is as natural and instinctive as breathing. Even when asleep humans communicate. Look at someone when they are in slumber and see how their face and sleeping position betray the various nocturnal thoughts of their sub-conscious minds. Death is the only human condition in which communication cannot operate in some form.

The fact that communication is so easy and instinctive is very positive news for the student of acting – for actors aim to communicate

'The chair' is a lonely place to be.

truthfully and naturally as part of their job. However, it is not your own thoughts and feeling that you are required to communicate when you act, but those of the character you are playing. It may well be instinctive to show personal mental processes, but what of those belonging to the fictitious creations of your colleagues, the playwrights?

Imagine your mind as if it were a computer. A computer can do a multitude of things but essentially it remains the same; its hardware can only function as it has been designed to do. What changes is the program that the computer is running. Acting is about meta-phorically running a different software program. If you can think the thoughts that match the words given to your character by the playwright but allow your body and voice to express these thoughts as normal – as if they were your own – your acting will always appear natural, spontaneous, real and truthful. The thoughts and intentions of your character may not be yours, but they must come alive through you in a wholly organic way. Audiences want to see something lifelike with which they can identify at an instinctive level in order to 'suspend their disbelief' for the duration of the play. If you can supply this you are more than halfway to winning their applause.

DO NOT PRETEND

But exactly how easy is this to do? The problem is that when you pretend to think the thoughts of others as if they were your own (and then do so again and again in rehearsal and performance), all of your natural ability to communicate may desert you. You may become unnatural because you are in an unnatural situation. The key here is the word 'pretend'. You must not 'pretend', you must 'be'; you must not replicate reality, you must create it. Pretending leads to wooden and stilted acting, and it must be firmly rejected by every student of acting. So you must start now to learn how to act without pretence.

THE WHOLE TRUTH AND NOTHING BUT THE TRUTH

The volunteer returns to their lonely chair (it should be the same person) and repeats the previous exercise. However, this time, instead of trying to do nothing they are instructed to think about an imaginary situation of their own choosing that would involve them sitting for at least sixty seconds without speaking. Here are some examples:

- in a dentist's or doctor's waiting room
- waiting for a job interview
- watching a film or television programme
- listening to somebody who is talking to you – a lecture, a telling-off or a story
- at home awaiting the return of a loved one
- feeling too ill to stand up.

During the one minute, with the onlookers carefully scrutinizing as before, the volunteer must put themselves into their imaginary situation, let the relevant thoughts that the situation conjures pass through their mind and then allow the body to communicate as it wants. The key word here is 'allow'. The volunteer should not try to stop any look, gesture or movement that may occur. However, they must not *make* these looks, gestures and movements happen in order to try to *show* what they are thinking and what

QUICK START GUIDE TO ACTING

1. Being Alive on Stage

When acting, try to develop an attitude of mind that will lead you towards truth and reality. Do not think of your work in terms of pretending, fabricating or simulating. See yourself as a craftsperson who works with the mediums of integrity, realism, actuality and authenticity to create characters that really live and breath. You, after all, are alive and, as it is from you that each of your characters spring, there is no reason why they should not be alive too.

Often, the very process of studying and rehearsing a role can kill the character, for you can easily fall into the trap of predictability and lack of spontaneity. This can be avoided simply by having the right mindset. Live on stage as you live in life. Try not to feel too safe, prepared or set in a particular way of doing things. Feel open and free and ready to move where the performance takes you. Ironically, the ability to do this stems from the acquiring of technique and the persistent practising of it, but your aim in all your acting should be to create work that is truly alive. Your characters are dead on the page and your job is to give them life on the stage – by sharing your life, your *real* life, with them, not by trying to pretend they exist or treating them as puppets. Although this can be easier said than done, half the battle is simply finding the right way of thinking and banishing the very idea that you are pretending.

their situation is. In fact, they should not worry what is communicated to the onlookers

An actor must never 'demonstrate'.

at all, for this would be to perform rather than act. To give an example: if the situation involves the volunteer in a feeling of impatient waiting for something, the last thing they should do is to look pointedly at their watch and grimace. The trick is to let the communication flow naturally from thoughts and feelings. The volunteer should just keep thinking, stay relaxed within, and then they will communicate quite naturally without being particularly aware of what they are actually doing in this respect.

The onlookers are asked, as before, to state what they have witnessed. They will not necessarily guess the exact situation (neither should they, as that is not the point), but, if the exercise has worked properly, they should have seen communication traits leading them to identify broad thoughts and emotions connected to the situation.

Now the onlookers are asked the vital question: did what they witnessed during this one-minute scene (for that is now what it has become) seem natural? or, did the volunteer look as if they were deliberately trying to show

their thoughts? The aim here is to communicate freely and openly but without resorting to 'mugging' or overplaying of any kind.

There is one more question for the group to answer: did they see any of the involuntary communication traits from the previous part of the exercise (when the volunteer was just asked to do nothing)? All of these previous observances should have disappeared, except any that were relevant to the imaginary situation.

PROPER ACTING

This exercise, although extremely simple, is designed to focus your mind on what acting is and what it is not. Proper acting is far closer to a normal way of existence than pretending and demonstrating. You have proved to yourself that, provided you think clearly and trust yourself to respond honestly and easily to your thoughts and feelings, you can appear natural and real despite those very thoughts and feelings being totally imaginary and false.

An instinctive movement can be extremely telling.

You can trick the body into believing that the impulses and instructions it is receiving from the mind are real, with the result that it just gets on with things as usual. Hundreds of tiny little communication traits appear (an inclination of the head, a hesitation within a gesture, a slight lowering of the eyes, a raising of an eyebrow and many millions more), all of which could not be thought about, prepared and rehearsed in advance. If you consciously tried to do these things you would look false and awkward. If you are acting properly you should not even be aware of them.

Of course, there is a lot more to acting than sitting in a chair. There is walking and talking to master as well – not to mention characterization and emotion – but there is plenty of time to worry about these. For the moment, you have learnt of, experienced and understood real and proper acting at its basic level.

If you are working with others, make sure that you all have a go at being 'in the chair'. Get to feel for yourselves when you are acting naturally and when you are 'forcing' the communication. It will come and go, and each exercise will be a mixture of both, but the

QUICK START GUIDE TO ACTING

2. Living from Moment to Moment

When acting, don't try to *show* your audience the character and what they are like. Just try as hard as you can to be the character, think their thoughts and feel their feelings as they live their particular lives. Study the part and the play, and be truthful to your interpretation of them. An audience gets to know a character by watching them over the course of a play, seeing what they do, listening to what they say and observing other characters' reactions to them. Therefore, you do not have to present the character as a whole at any given moment of the play. You must not inform the audience of the character, but allow them to inform themselves by watching you, as the character, live from moment to moment. Remember never to demonstrate the part. Have faith in the integrity of your acting and trust that your characterizations will express themselves naturally.

A proper actor never plays a scene the same way twice.

important thing is to learn to feel when it is right and when it is wrong – that is all that is needed at this stage.

AN EVER-CHANGING PERFORMANCE

When you are acting properly each of your performances will be different. Each night, although you say the same words and essentially do the same actions, the way you say and do them will never quite be the same. You will be 'living' the part in a very real sense and as you move from one moment to the next your body and voice will respond as uniquely to the moment as they do in real life.

Because of this, you must never 'hang on' to any particular communication devices. That sly little scratch of the nose that worked so well last night, might not work as well tonight. Last night it was 'real', tonight you are 'trying to make it real' – there is a difference. In other words, when you act you have to trust. You have to trust yourself to play the scene, let it pass through your head, and allow what happens to happen. Being real is not safe – it is a step into the unknown, and because of this it may go wrong. If you want to be a good actor, you will have to accept the fact that sometimes you will be bad. However, at other times (hopefully the majority of times) you will be magnificent.

PRACTICAL THOUGHTS

There can be no doubt that in order to achieve your goal of 'reality acting' you must be well prepared. The audience will know when you are not acting properly. They won't necessarily be aware of why they know this. They will simply think, 'I don't believe that performance' – and that, to an actor, is a painful insult indeed.

However, part of being well prepared is realizing that being truthful is not your only consideration on stage. Being a good actor is not all about reality and truth. There are very practical things you need to think about that have nothing to do with the integrity of the part you are playing, such as: remembering your lines; not falling over the furniture; and acting at the right pace. Be warned, if you start to get pretentious over your quest for reality in your acting, you will end up falling off the stage.

Good communication between actor and director is invaluable.

A PRACTICAL APPROACH

So you will need a technique, a way of thinking, that will allow you to achieve the truth you need while still being able to execute the very technically demanding job of navigating your way through a play performance. You need a way of being able to stand offstage awaiting your entrance cue, trying to remember if you turned the gas off at home, and then walking straight into the scene as if you had been your character since its conception. You need a way of taking very specific notes from a director and making them work for your character. Later, in Chapter 4, you will learn about the 'Two-Brain Theory', which will supply these needs perfectly. In the meantime, there are more acting fundamentals to learn first.

3   THE ACTOR ALONE

A PLAN OF ACTION

The title of this chapter suggests a study of those moments when you are alone on the stage, sharing your thoughts with the audience or, indeed, yourself. This is true, but what you will learn here will also have relevance to the acting you do with others. Before you can start rehearsing any scene with fellow actors you must have a very clear idea in your head what that scene is about for you personally and how you intend to approach the action and dialogue moment by moment. As you will learn in Chapter 4, this may well change dramatically when you start to interact with the other characters in the scene, and good acting is about being open and responsive to these changes. However, you must begin with a very clear plan of your thoughts and intentions throughout; you must start from a position of clarity. Acting is about living the part and the text 'in the moment', and to do this effectively you must have a strong concept of how you will move forwards in the scene. More importantly, you need to be able to progress in a way that truthfully and realistically engages your ability to think naturally and spontaneously, even

OPPOSITE: **An actor's journey starts in his mind.**

though you are, in reality, following a pre-determined plan. You need to be able to follow a clearly defined path while making it appear that you are walking that route for the first time.

This process needs to be started in a very simple and basic way, far removed from all the complexities of high drama and passionate emotion. The grass roots of acting are very 'down to earth', and so for the time being you must continue to remain extremely pedestrian in your thinking.

FINDING YOUR PEN

Imagine that you want to write a letter and you have lost your pen, but you know that you have absentmindedly put the pen down somewhere in the room. Now imagine what it would be like finding it. Think about how you would go about the task; how you would think; how thorough you would be. Don't think of yourself as another person – imagine yourself searching for the pen and how you might look to an outside observer while doing so. Try to get a clear picture in your mind of the pattern of your thoughts and how the speed of them may change as you move from place to place in the room and encounter likely and less likely places for the illusive pen to be.

The choice of a boring object such as a pen is deliberate. There is no high drama here, just a normal, everyday irritation. You should be able to perceive your reactions to this simple, if annoying, task easily and the manner in which you would approach it. If you were able to watch yourself looking for this pen, you would see a variety of movements, expressions and small gestures that would be communicating a variety of thoughts and intentions. In truth, what you would be observing is someone living a part of their real life quite naturally and spontaneously. Admittedly, this would be a very ordinary and boring part of their life, but it would be a real part; it would look real because it would be real.

In order to get a better picture of how a human being appears when they are looking for something you need to see it for real. Hide a pen in a room and ask a friend to try to find it for you. Explain to them that this is not acting and that you are simply asking them to find something that is hidden – there is no pretending involved at all. Carefully observe them, watching for signs of how they are 'thinking through' the process and how this communicates itself to you. They will not appear entirely natural because they will be aware of you watching them, but it will be very close to a slice of real life.

THE SEARCH BECOMES A SCENE

Having established how a very ordinary task, like looking for a pen, appears when it is real, you need to discover if that reality can be replicated when it is not. In other words, can you make looking for, and then finding, a pen seem natural, spontaneous and (most importantly) truthful, when you actually know where it is? The answer to this question is 'yes', provided it is approached correctly.

Hide a pen somewhere in a room and set yourself the task of finding it within the space of approximately one minute. As you do this, try to put the pen's location and your eventual discovery of it to the back of your mind and concentrate on the processes of searching. Allow your thoughts to progress naturally and freely as you search the room. Do not think about what you look like. You are not trying to 'show' someone that you are really looking, you are just trying actually to look. Focus on your thoughts and intentions and let your body do what it will.

Now ask your friend to do this too. Show them where the pen is hidden and then ask them to find it as naturally as they can. Impress upon them that they must not try to 'perform' the actions of looking for the pen, but must simply try to replicate them. As you observe them, watch out for signs of 'demonstrating'; they may well be tempted to indulge in what they consider to be appropriate facial expressions and gestures, such as immense frowns of concentration and gestures of feigned frustration. These will look false because they are; what will look real is an ability to think as near naturally as possible. Keep trying this yourself and begin to get a feel for when you are behaving naturally and when you are demonstrating. In terms of expression and gesture 'less is more'; clarity of thought and progression of thought are what are truly important here. If possible, ask your friend to watch you and give you constructive feedback on your progress.

In essence, you have now turned looking for a pen into a scene and you have become the playwright. The situation is totally false because you know where the pen is and you have set an approximate time for its search and discovery. However, this does not mean that it will necessarily appear false because the processes of searching and finding may still be real if you let them; as long as you forget about demonstrating and think hard about living in the moment you will tap into your normal and instinctive thought patterns even though you are now, in effect, 'playing a scene'. Gradually, you will become more and more accustomed to the feel and rhythm of this, and you will begin instinctively to look for the pen as if the search were for real.

THE REVERSAL OF LIFE

The problem that all actors face is that playwrights turn life upside down; they reverse it. Instead of events moving forwards towards conclusions that can never be certain, the actor is required to move along a preordained line towards an ending that is certain. Because of this, you will find, if you are not careful, that you are playing a scene 'backwards'. Nothing will seem real or spontaneous because you are, in essence, always moving from one certainty to another towards an outcome that has already been decided; from an action you knew you would take to an action you know you will take next; from a word you knew you would say to a word that you know must be spoken. The very act of writing a play does this – it predetermines actions and words and, as such, is completely opposite to life. To put it simply, the words and actions come before the thoughts and intentions.

Your job as an actor is to turn the scene back up the right way; to reinstate the normal progression of life and return the scene to naturalism. This can only be done by making sure that you are clear about the thoughts and intentions that you must have in the scene and ensuring they come first. It is possible to spout lots of sentences that have been written for you and for them to mean absolutely nothing in your head; or at least nothing that is relevant to what you are actually saying. This must not happen; everything you say must mean something to you and must be the result of a natural impetus. The key to success here is to think and live as near to your normal state as possible and not to see what you are doing and saying as something

outside of yourself. Whatever character you may be playing, and however defined that character may be, all of their thoughts must be organically and naturally yours. While 'looking for the pen', you have not been required to play a character at all and the scenario has been extremely straightforward. However, it is possible to stretch yourself further by making the exercise harder.

PANIC SEARCH

Repeat the one-minute searching scene only, but this time exchanging the pen for a set of

---

QUICK START GUIDE TO ACTING

4. Clear Thoughts and Intentions

Break down every piece of acting you do into a clear and straightforward picture of what your character is trying to do, why they are trying to do it and their resulting thoughts. Your guide for this process will be the words that the playwright has given you, but it is your job to process what you think lies behind these words so that, when you bring them to the stage, they are not only spoken naturalistically but are accompanied by other, equally naturalistic, physical communication devices such as gesture and facial expression.

In order for your acting to appear real to an audience it must have its origins in real thought and intention. Trust yourself to be clear enough in your thinking for your body and voice to respond quite naturally. In this way, you will not only present characters that really 'live', but you will be able to access the great wealth of your own personality in order to give your acting truth.

Emotion takes the acting process to a higher level.

keys and elaborate the process by playing the following imaginary scenario:

You are locked in the room and only by finding the keys will you be able to make your escape. The door or doors of the room are solid and any windows are reinforced and impossible to break – only the keys can release you. In the middle of the room is a large bomb ... and it is ticking! On the side of the bomb is a timer, showing numbers counting down towards zero; you only have a minute to live inside the room. Find the key.

Of course, drama has now been added to the scene, making it not only more interesting and exciting, but potentially more complex to act. You now have much more acting to do and it is acting that involves your heart as well as your mind. However, you are still playing yourself, so your reactions to the situation can be your own. You may remain reasonably calm and logical, or you may run into a blind panic; whatever, there will be an underlying feeling of fear and tension within you that was not there previously.

The important thing here is that you remain truthful and real; that you continue to process your actions naturally and allow your emotions to emerge realistically. Some people find this quite hard to achieve at first and find themselves demonstrating wildly. However, others learn that the added content of the scene helps them to focus their mind more strongly and to discover more realism than when the scene was quite ordinary. Again, watch a colleague, and have them watch you, in order to analyse your own abilities in this respect. Try to really feel the emotions and let your content and speed of thought reflect them. Do not look at this as a performance; how real you *appear* is not as important as how real you *feel* at this stage. You must convince yourself about the situation so that you can play it realistically; an actor cannot expect an audience to have belief in what they do if they do not believe it themselves.

ADDING WORDS AND FINDING SPONTANEITY

You must now consider a similar process, but this time with words added to action. Read very carefully the following speech from a play and learn it as accurately as you can. The situation is that of a boss showing a new employee around an office and takes the form of a monologue spoken by the boss to the employee as they move around:

> This open area is the main part of the office – this is where most of the work gets done. As you can see, there are filing cabinets everywhere but we are going to move them all together against this wall when we get the time. The photocopier is in the corner here – it

needs servicing about once a month. Be careful, I think someone's spilt some water down here and it might be slippery – I'll mop it up in a minute. This tray is where we put any dockets to be sent down to dispatch – it seems to be overflowing at the moment – if you want anything done do it yourself! This coffee machine is broken at the moment but there's a kettle in the side office if you get desperate. This is your desk – nice and near the window, which is always an advantage I think. At least this room is big and airy – there's nothing worse than being claustrophobic, especially when you're under pressure, like we are in here most of the time. Right, well, if you'll follow me I'll take you down to Invoicing.

The main object when playing this speech is to achieve spontaneity. An actor speaks a succession of words that have been said time and again, but which must be spoken as if for the first time and as if just thought of. Things are made a little easier for you here by the fact that *the boss* may well have done this 'tour' before (perhaps many times), so there will be a small element of natural repetition. However, your job is to bring the speech alive from the page and make it sound 'of the moment' using the same method of realistic thinking as before.

THE MAP

Begin by structuring in your mind how you will move through this speech mentally. Work out what is going to make you say certain things and how the visual stimulus of the office (albeit imaginary) might lead you from thought to thought. Consider too the things said that this character intended to say and those that are prompted by the various stimuli of the moment. In other words, create a very generalized map for yourself that will act as a guide from one end of the speech to the other.

The following is by way of example, but will, of course, differ from your own personal plan. The words in brackets are not to be spoken but are a guide to one possible set of thought processes that aim towards creating a spontaneous delivery of the text. They are roughly positioned before the words they trigger:

(*usual start – said this before*) This open area is the main part of the office – (*usual little dig at those in high places*) this is where most of the work gets done. (*the place is a mess – apologetic*) As you can see, there are filing cabinets everywhere (*don't put them off*) but we are going to move them all together against this wall (*if we ever get round to it*) when we get the time. (*what to say next – see the photocopier – new thought*) The photocopier is in the corner here – (*sudden extra thought – amusement*) it needs servicing about once a month. (*surprise and concern – sudden thought*) Be careful, I think someone's spilt some water down here and it might be slippery – (*in passing – throwaway thought*) I'll mop it up in a minute. (*see tray – important point springs to mind*) This tray is where we put any dockets to be sent down to dispatch – (*mind drifts, annoyance at who might be responsible*) it seems to be overflowing at the moment – (*sudden funny thought*) if you want anything done do it yourself! (*what next? – think of machine*) This coffee machine is broken at the moment (*throwaway – not important*) but there's a kettle in the side office if you get desperate. (*have been working towards this important point – in mind from start*) This is your desk – (*pleased – selling point*) nice and near the window, which is always an advantage I think. (*sudden thought leading from last*) At least this room is big and airy – there's nothing worse than being claustrophobic, (*going well – thought

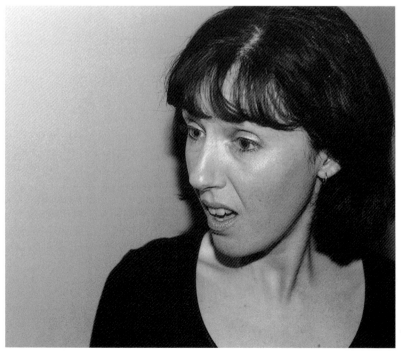

An actor should move forward through the scene, from thought to thought.

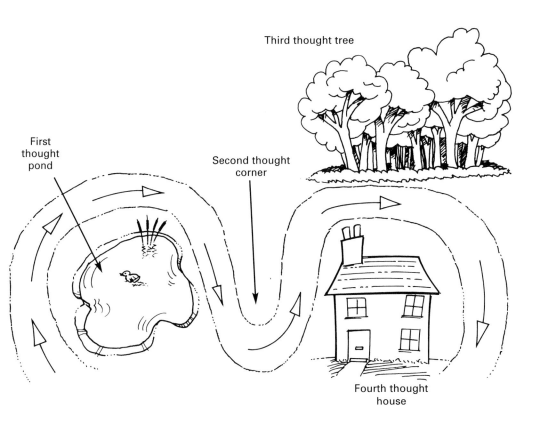

An actor should construct a basic map of thoughts and intentions.

building confidently) especially when you're under pressure, like we are in here most of the time. (*anything else? – no, move on*) Right, well, if you'll follow me I'll take you down to Invoicing.

Thus you create your very basic map of thought. It is not your intention actually to think these thoughts word for word before you say the next piece of text, but to use them as a general guide to your way of thinking at each stage. Never try to be aware of actual thoughts in terms of specific words when you are acting, for you are rarely aware of thought in this way

in life. Your map is purely a guide to set you thinking in the right way – the thinking itself will manifest itself more as feelings of intention, rather than actual mental commands.

It is also important to know that this is just a starting point and not a rigid format. In the next chapter you will experience how playing a speech like this with another actor (in this case the new employee) will change the way you think at different times, even though the other actor may not actually speak. For the time being though, practise this by yourself, imagining an employee and using the largest room in your home as an imaginary office.

QUICK START GUIDE TO ACTING

5. 'Thinking' in Sporting Terms

It can sometimes be helpful, when acting, to think of your thoughts in rather the same way as you might think of hitting a ball with a racket. Firstly, the racket is taken back in preparation for the shot, then the ball is hit and, finally, the player completes the shot by 'following through' with the racket. The natural process of thinking follows a similar procedure:

1. The thought starts to form – it begins to show in the face and body.
2. The thought arrives fully – the word or words are spoken.
3. The thought continues (the follow-through) for a while, still showing in facial expression or gesture.

A very basic, but illustrative, example for you to experiment with is this:

1. **A** has an important thought; he takes in a breath and makes very purposeful eye contact with **B**.
2. The words are said.
3. A continues to look at **B** and raises his eyebrows and inclines his head to con-solidate the point he has just made.

Of course, in sport the degree of preparation and follow-through varies according to the type of shot to be played. Thus in acting thoughts will have different amounts of the same depending upon the speed of the thought in question and the next following it: in effect, the principle remains constant. Just remember that a thought never exists in isolation within a word or words. Think on stage as you do in life.

SOME IMPORTANT POINTS

Remember when attempting this speech that you are trying to be as spontaneous as possible. As you follow your map you will find that the speed and intensity of your thoughts will vary. Allow this to dictate the pace, fluidity and emphasis of your speaking, and the formulation and intensity of your movement, facial expression and gestures. The keyword here (as always) is 'allow'; do not force anything to happen as you will become stilted, measured and predictable.

If you do have a go at this, you will find it much easier to be spontaneous if you learn the speech rather than read it. This is simply because the process of remembering is much closer to original thought than the process of reading. The speech should be learnt word for word and not paraphrased. This is so that you fit your thoughts to the playwright's words and not the other way round. In this way, you will be training yourself to be a 'classical' actor; in other words, an actor who can make any text real and spontaneous without altering it.

THINKING THE EXTRA BITS

The last point is worthy of a little expansion. Have another look at this one line from the speech: 'Be careful, I think someone's spilt some water down here and it might be slippery.' It may well be that as an actor saying this line you feel that the impetus for it is suddenly realizing that you are standing in a wet puddle. This is fine and is a good way to proceed into the line from the line before. This may in turn lead you to an overwhelming desire to curse before you say the line. For example: 'Damn! Be careful, I think someone's spilt some water down here and it might be slippery.' However, the exercise will not allow you to add this extra word. There is very little wrong with doing so (and in some productions it would be encouraged to ad lib in this way), but it goes against the general principle of the disciplined, classical acting that you are trying to achieve at this early stage; you must learn the rules before you may break them. But that does not mean that the curse cannot be presented in another way. If you experiment, you will find that you are able to 'think' the word 'damn' (or another like it) into the saying of the words 'Be careful'. You will be able to make these words have a double purpose: the obvious meaning of 'watch out', and in addition a parallel meaning of 'what a nuisance'. Try this and listen to the way your voice can naturally express what is in your head, whatever you are saying.

This incorporating and layering of different thoughts into words and phrases is something we do all the time in real life. However, the bad actor forgets this and irons out all the complexities and idiosyncrasies of com-munication into an unnatural flatness. You must allow the brain (with its ability to communicate on many levels) to function in the same way when you are acting as it does in your life as a whole. Acting is simply about doing what you do supremely well anyway.

THE NEW THOUGHT DEVICE

In your daily life you will have experienced the sensation of talking to someone or doing something and suddenly having a completely new (and sometimes quite unrelated) thought. This causes you quickly to alter the way you are speaking or moving: you change gear and your energy level fluctuates. This can be a very effective device to create naturalism in your acting and enable you to realistically, but quite dramatically, vary your pace and attack. Be careful, though, to maintain continuity of thought. Even an unrelated new thought will always have a trigger – either something you

have just said or seen that makes a connection, however tenuous. These triggers must be played in order to keep this device truthful.

Return to the office monologue again and experiment with using this New Thought Device in order to be even more naturalistic. You will find this speech particularly rich in terms of potential places to use it as well as triggers to instigate it realistically.

SUBTEXT

Subtext is often referred to as the hidden but real thoughts behind the obvious meanings of words and actions. However, it is not necessarily helpful to consider this in isolation from the techniques of naturalistic thinking as a whole. You must learn to be clear in your thinking and intentions in a scene, although your thoughts may rarely fit the most obvious definitions of what you are saying and doing. Text and subtext exist together in a whole that is 'particular thought'. If you know why you are saying and doing things on stage, then there need not be a clear definition of where text ends and subtext begins. Identifying subtext will certainly be part of your preparatory work for a scene, but the playing of it should naturally incorporate itself into your technique without causing you to approach it in isolation.

By way of example, consider the following very short scene:

Sally: Do you like the dress I'm wearing?

Joe: Yes, it's beautiful.

Sally's line could contain the subtext 'Do you love me?' and Joe's may contain 'I love you very much' by way of reply. However, if used in this way, the scene would be so dominated by the subtext that nothing else need be played. The basic definition of this question and answer will

Text and subtext work together – 'I hate you!'/'I'm scared!'

look after itself – your thoughts will be full of the subtext. In fact, it is practically impossible to play this scene 'straight', as exchanges of this nature will always have some significant meaning beyond words.

For examples try playing the scene four times with different subtexts each time. Use the original words but 'play' the following:

Sally: Do you think I've spent too much money?

Joe: Yes, but it's OK

Sally: I don't like this dress; I wish I hadn't bought it

Joe: I'm too busy to think about dresses.

Sally: Do you know my lover bought me this dress?

Joe: You are so stupid.

Sally: I'm really pleased with this dress.

Joe: I want you to be happy.

In the last of these the subtext has practically evaporated into the text. However, there is no difference – the words are simply vessels for the thoughts and their actual meaning becomes almost irrelevant. There is no perceivable version of this scene where the question and answer it contains can stand alone – text and subtext fuse together to give life and meaning.

To test this further, play the four subtexts again, but this time do not use words: make what you think are appropriate noises for each thought and intention. You should still be able to make the meaning of the scene reasonably apparent and you will learn that the words are just shapes without any life of their own – until you give it to them.

EMOTIONAL MEMORY

As an actor you are in the unique position of being able to use every experience you have ever had in your work. Everything that happens to you in life can be drawn upon to inform and illuminate your acting – giving it realism and truth. This is called your Emotional Memory, and you should think of it as a bank in which you deposit experiences and observations from your daily life, to be drawn upon when needed.

However, it is important that Emotional Memory is used properly. If you were playing a scene in which your character was traumatized by the death of a close relative or friend, it would be inappropriate to remember how you felt as a child when your budgerigar died and to use this as a direct substitute in your mind. To do this would not be acting, as you would not be playing the situation as written but a completely different one. Instead, you should draw upon your childhood experience, along with others, to 'tap into' the feelings and emotions required generally, without using them specifically. In this way, each and every minute of your life contributes to this invaluable resource, which, as it grows, allows you to act more truthfully with every part that you play.

In order to be proactive in the compiling of your Emotional Memory it is important that you live your life to the full – do not waste a single day in experiencing as much of life as you can, and see everything that happens to you as a positive contribution to your success as an actor.

4 ACTING WITH OTHERS

A TEAM GAME

One of the most important truths about acting is that an actor is only ever as good (or, for that matter, as bad) as the other actors on stage. While acting is often viewed as competitive, it is, in reality, one of the most essentially cooperative activities that exist. However talented you may be, however honed and refined your technique, you will always be dependent upon your fellows for the ultimate quality of your performance.

True, there are occasions when you will be alone upon the stage, but the majority of your time will be spent acting with others and you must learn to 'feed' their performances, as you require them to 'feed' yours. In life, much of what you say and do is determined as a reaction to the words and actions of those you are in contact with: you respond to them and they, in turn, respond to you. All of your communication devices are subconsciously and instinctively linked to this interplay, and so the way you look and sound at any particular moment is inextricably entwined with other people. It is not only essential that this process is closely replicated in acting for the sake of spontaneity and naturalism – it is also the very 'life blood' of proper acting itself.

*OPPOSITE: **An actor is only as good as her fellow actors.***

ACTING IN REAL TIME

When an actor is engaged in, say, a duologue with another, it becomes very easy for that actor to become a slave to predetermined reactions. After all, the play has been written down, it already exists and the actor knows exactly what is to happen or to be said next. Generally this is unavoidable and, indeed, desirable – the actor will have mapped out the scene and will know the basic reactions that the scene requires. However, those reactions must happen in practice and not in theory. In other words, despite a previous knowledge of what is to come, the actor must really listen, watch and respond to everything that happens – as it happens. As an example of this, look at the following four lines of a duologue:

A: What was that? I heard a noise.

B: Calm down! It's just your imagination.

A: Will you listen to me for once? There's somebody downstairs – I know there is.

B: I'd better go and have a look then, hadn't I?

Were this to be taken from a real scene in a play then the basic attitudes of each character and their reaction to each other and the situation would be worked out in rehearsal. However, in performance, the exchange must still happen in

'What was that? I heard a noise.'

'real time'. It may well be that, at one particular performance, **A** may say one of the lines just a little differently than in previous performances; if **B** is really listening, their reply will vary a little too. This may well be an imperceptible difference and the actor will probably not be aware of it, but the important thing is that they will have really replied to their colleague rather than replying in an entirely preordained way. Although a seemingly imperceptible moment like this may not be at all important, it is when lots of such moments are joined together that acting comes alive; it ceases to exist on the page and becomes a living entity in its own right. When members of an audience watch

moment-by-moment reactions and interactions they become convinced of a suspended reality; when they watch actors merely 'speaking lines' in turn they become convinced only of pretence and sham.

Try repeatedly running through this short duologue with a colleague. Although you will quickly establish the general pattern of the scene, you will be surprised as to how it will change and develop with each attempt – provided you ensure that you observe and listen to each other as if you had no idea what you were about to say and do. You will find that the scene, albeit short and simple, will start to exist in a way that neither of you is fully

An actor must really listen and watch.

controlling – this is proper acting.

THE COURAGEOUS ACTOR

Acting in this way is very brave. It means that the actor is not fully in control of what is happening to her or him. They will certainly know their lines and have a technical control over what they are doing, but they will never be quite certain of how they will actually act the scene or, indeed, how good or bad it will be. To be a good actor you will have to embrace this danger. To be good at acting you must take risks; you must work hard in rehearsal and work out the basics of what you want to achieve, but then you must go out on the stage and let it happen. You must allow yourself to be as vulnerable on stage as you are in life. Your performance will be totally bound up not only in your own contribution, but also in that of your fellow actors and the second-by-second unfolding of events in the play. You will be technically in command, but artistically you will be 'riding' the play like a wave.

THE DIFFERENCE BETWEEN AN ACTOR AND A PERFORMER

Although acting is often referred to as performing in the sense that it is an activity which engages you in 'a performance', there is

35

a big difference between an actor and a performer in the way they approach their work.

A performer's instinct is to assume a persona and a method of presentation. A performer analyses how best to communicate his or her material and then finds a particular voice, physicality and manner through which to portray that material. In a sense, a performer 'puts on' a performance rather like putting on a coat. An actor looks at things differently – he or she is in the business of recreating reality, not assuming it. Everything an actor does while playing a role should stem from a truthful reaction not only to the text, but also to each and every stimulus that is produced from the communal input of all the other actors. An actor does not 'put on' or 'wear' anything, but rather exists on stage in exactly the way the play is leading them to be at each particular moment.

Of course, most performers are removed from the kind of work that actors do anyway – they are comedians, singers or dancers perhaps. But the performance skills they use can be seen often in so-called 'acting' and are a poor substitute for the real thing. To illustrate the point for yourself, think of a comedian when involved in a comedy sketch. They are using text, speech and movement as an actor does, but they are performing and not acting. Their voice, movement and expression is set in an appropriate way. This may be perfectly adequate for the purposes of the sketch, but an actor would be seeking a more organic technique for the long term. If you were to watch an actor playing the same sketch you would notice the difference.

Sustaining true acting is not easy and you must not be too hard on yourself as you try to practise it. During a play you may find that you are acting properly for 20 per cent of the time and performing for the other 80 per cent. This is not a bad average. As your technical ability increases, you will find yourself truly acting

more and more. Performing is your 'bottom line' – your adequate and acceptable norm; proper acting, when it happens, is what will make you good. When it happens often, you will be very good.

STARTING TO ACT WITH OTHERS

Look once more at the following text from the last chapter and relearn it if required:

This open area is the main part of the office – this is where most of the work gets done. As you can see, there are filing cabinets everywhere but we are going to move them all together against this wall when we get the time. The photocopier is in the corner here – it needs servicing about once a month. Be careful, I think someone's spilt some water down here and it might be slippery – I'll mop it up in a minute. This tray is where we put any dockets to be sent down to dispatch – it seems to be overflowing at the moment – if you want anything done do it yourself! This coffee machine is broken at the moment but there's a kettle in the side office if you get desperate. This is your desk – nice and near the window, which is always an advantage I think. At least this room is big and airy – there's nothing worse than being claustrophobic, especially when you're under pressure, like we are in here most of the time. Right, well, if you'll follow me I'll take you down to Invoicing.

Start by recalling your basic map of thoughts and intentions that you created in the previous chapter. Play the speech through again using this and enjoy the feeling that you are now quickly acquiring the technique needed to make the words live truthfully.

You now need to enlist the help of a friend. Find a space that is as near to an office environment as possible in which to rehearse the speech. There should be furniture and objects that approximate those that are mentioned in the text. Your friend's role is simple – to play the person who is being shown around by you. Your friend does not have to speak, but does have to listen to what you say and look at what you ask them to. As you play the speech, relate to them as if the situation were real. Already you will find that the organic feedback you receive from your friend's expressions and body language will begin subtly to affect the way you play the speech. There will not be enormous changes, but, if you allow some sort of real relationship to develop with your partner, the scene will begin to become more real than it was before.

While doing this it is vital that you take your time: do not let the text rush you. Place emphasis on eye contact and a general feeling of empathy with your partner. Because an actor's first introduction to any particular piece of acting is as text written on a page, it is understandable that the speaking of that text can become a driving factor in its performance. However, this can lead to a lifeless and unreal rendition of the words. True, the words are the usual starting point, but they lead the actor to compile thoughts and intentions; these in turn lead to a wholeness in the performance. This wholeness is made up of looking, listening, moving, facial expressions, gestures and, of course, speaking, but the speaking is not necessarily more important than any of the others: living is not just about speech, neither should acting be.

It is now time to make things a little harder. Perform the scene again with your friend, but this time ask them to improvise comments about some of the things that they are shown. These can be good or bad comments and they do not have to be spoken for every item. You must remain 'on text', which should be possible provided you instruct your partner to restrict their input to comments and not to ask you a direct question. Be open to what they say, allow it to affect you and, more importantly, the way in which you continue to conduct the imaginary office tour. If they are positive and complimentary in their remarks this will probably encourage you in your enthusiasm; if they are negative and critical a reverse result will start to manifest. However, do not force these reactions; just allow yourself and your performance to be affected by this other person. You will start to find that the text is fast becoming the only constant factor, and that your life around the text will be shaping itself naturally and in an ever more malleable form. You will be moving further away from 'performing' and towards 'acting'.

'This area is the main part of the office.'

An Experiment in Communal Spontaneity

The stimulation and spontaneous reaction that can be gained from working with other actors can be ultimately experienced by working with a partner on the following duologue based upon an interrogation scene:

A: Tell me about what you heard your brother say.

B: My brother?

A: Yes, you told me you overheard him on the telephone.

B: Oh, I see what you mean – he was just telling his wife that he was going to be home late, that's all.

A: He wasn't shouting, arguing with her in any way?

B: No, he loved Sarah; they never argued about anything.

A: Are you sure?

B: Yes, quite sure.

A: You didn't get the impression that she was giving him a hard time about being late.

B: No.

A: It would have been reasonable – it was past seven and he had been due in just after five as usual.

B: It wasn't his fault. We had been very busy at the office that day ... a family business doesn't run itself, you know ... the accounts were due the following week. Of course, if he'd known she was in danger he wouldn't have left her at all ... he would have ...

A: I understand that this is very difficult for you but I want you to think very clearly – did you hear him say anything on the phone that was unusual?

B: No, of course not. It was a perfectly normal conversation.

A: Then why did you mention it to me? You must have suspected something.

B: Nothing at all. Why should I?

A: Look, why don't you just tell me the truth and get it over with. You'll feel much better if you do.

B: I am telling you the truth.

A: Are you?

B: Yes.

A: Are you really?

B: Yes, I am.

You should begin by playing the part of **A** and your partner that of **B**. If you can commit the lines to memory, so much the better. Tell your partner to play their part in the way that feels right, but insist that they concentrate on listening and relating very closely to you in the scene and allow themselves to react accordingly. Now play the duologue through several times and each time change your approach to the scene. In one version you may be kindly and

The same scene may be played several different ways.

understanding; in another harsh and bullying; in another perhaps cynical and sarcastic. Don't give your partner too much time to think; each time you finish, start again immediately. The more you do this, the more instinctively and organically your partner's performance will change in reaction to the alterations in your own. The scene will take on life and colour and neither you nor your colleague will perform it the same way twice. Having experimented fully with this, reverse roles and see how even more variations can be created.

THE TRUTH AND THE TECHNICAL

The work that you have attempted so far (and particularly now that you have brought other actors into the equation) may well have created a conflict in your mind. This conflict pervades all acting, and its resolution ironically provides the magical key to all proper acting. It is the conflict between truth and technical requirements. Actors must be truthful and find a way of acting that is as close to life as possible, but they are also required to say and do predetermined things – technical requirements.

Directors also make technical requirements of actors. They may ask an actor to say a line louder or faster; to move in a certain way; to emphasize a particular word – these are all technical requirements that may pull the actor away from truth like a magnet. For example, you may have worked out the thoughts and motivation behind a particular line in a scene; you may have developed these truthfully in tandem with input from your fellow actors, and all is well. Suddenly, at one rehearsal, the

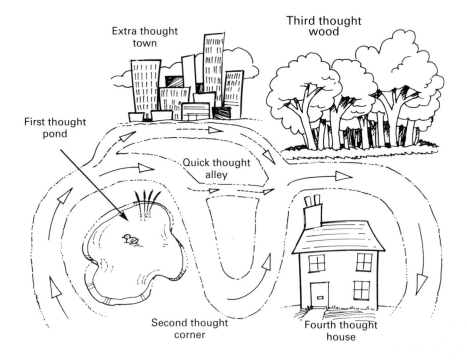

Extra thought
town

Third thought
wood

First thought
pond

Quick thought
alley

Second thought
corner

Fourth thought
house

The actor's map now contains detours and shortcuts.

QUICK START GUIDE TO ACTING

6. Concentrating

When working with other actors in a scene run through the following short checklist in your mind to make sure that you are acting properly:

1. Are you really listening to what is being said to you, or are you just relying on the fact that you know what will be said?

2. Are you really observing your fellow actors and making sure that you are aware of all their facial expressions and gestures, or are you just assuming that they will do exactly the same things as the last time you performed the scene?

3. Are you living in the moment of the scene so that your responses are organic and natural, or are you simply repeating your usual performance whatever?

4. Are you concentrating sufficiently to adapt the script if one of your fellow actors makes a mistake, or are you so much on autopilot that you might not even notice?

director asks you to play this line with more anger (a technical requirement), completely against your own instincts. The line starts to lose its naturalness and spontaneity, it ceases to be real and your acting, as you speak, starts to become wooden and awkward – in short, you have lost 'the truth' of the line. This moment of unreality will cause a 'hole' for you in the scene and this hole will start to spread in size – before long, the scene will start to become mechanical and lifeless.

Of course, this could be avoided by discussing your concerns with the director, and you should always feel able to talk freely in a rehearsal situation. However, sometimes it becomes inevitable that you must implement a technical requirement made upon you. Actors when working in television must often obey the most precise of technical directions. They may have to move to a specific spot, look in a particular direction at a given moment or step unnaturally close to another actor in order for both to be 'in shot'. Again, these technical requirements may be completely alien to the actor's perception of truthfully playing the scene.

It is not only outside forces that make technical demands of actors. Sometimes it is necessary for you to make such demands upon yourself. For instance, you may feel that a scene is moving too slowly and that you need to increase the pace in order to progress the scene and keep the audience's interest; however, this technical requirement of speed might not necessarily be in accord with your truthful instincts for the scene.

THE TWO-BRAIN THEORY

In order to solve this dilemma it is useful to think of the actor as having two brains. One of these brains is called the 'Truth Brain', the other the 'Technical Brain'. The Technical Brain identifies the technical requirements both of the play in the long term and of the

moment-to-moment acting in each scene. These requirements are vast in range and include such things as: remembering the exact words to say; varying the pace of the text; maintaining sufficient vocal projection; improvising if a colleague gets a line wrong; being in the right place at the right time; pausing before a certain word; structuring the emotion of a speech so that the climax occurs at the appropriate juncture; looking particularly shocked at the end of a scene to create a good curtain; speaking softly for dramatic effect but still allowing the audience to hear; getting to the door at just the right moment so as to exit quickly after a strong line; eating while talking; not obscuring a line of sight from your hand on a light switch to the lighting box so that the technician can coordinate the switching on of a light; and even making sure that an accidentally dropped object does not roll off the stage. It is irrelevant whether you or the director instigates these matters; they are of a technical nature and little to do with the truth of the acting involved. They therefore belong in the Technical Brain.

In order to maintain the naturalism and reality of the play, these technical problems must be properly handled or they will completely swamp all spontaneity and believability. This is achieved by passing every technical matter to the Truth Brain to be processed truthfully. By this means a technical necessity becomes a truthful desirability. This method can be best explained by four pertinent examples.

Example 1
An actor's Technical Brain identifies a technical need to pause before a certain word. The problem is passed to the Truth Brain, which solves the problem by finding a suitable reason or motivation, which matches the development of the character within the scene

at that particular moment. This might be in the form of a faltering voice due to excessive emotion, a momentary distraction prior to speaking the word, or a hesitation before saying something important. It is the job of the Truth Brain to select the most appropriate of these or another entirely. Whilst the decision for this kind of example may well have been taken in rehearsal, the Truth Brain must be ready to adapt and change the motivation in real time if required – it must keep the actor within the ongoing reality of the moment. For example, at one particular performance it may react to a stimulus a little differently and change the motivation of the pause to some extent. This is good, for it means that the acting will be alive and real – exactly what is trying to be achieved. It is important to

Dropping something accidentally on stage may be used to enhance reality.

remember that the technical requirement remains constant in the Technical Brain, but is ultimately changeable and adaptable as it is passed to the Truth Brain and becomes acting.

Example 2

An actor accidentally drops a prop on stage – perhaps a pen. The Technical Brain identifies the need to pick up the pen; this is because the actor may need to use the pen again later in the scene, but also because if the actor fails to pick it up the audience will wonder why and be distracted from the suspended reality of the scene. The Truth Brain accepts the challenge and motivates the action of picking up the pen according to the character being played and the situation at that moment of the scene: it may cause the actor to laugh, grimace or become unusually concerned by the action of retrieval; it may also dictate whether the actor should be swift or faltering in the execution of the move, according to the role. It will also decide if it is more natural to pause the dialogue or continue talking all the while; if talking does continue, the appropriate strain of the movement will be sounded in the voice.

Example 3

While acting in a thriller an actor is required to draw the attention of the audience to a particular clue. As this has everything to do with the plot and nothing to do with the realism of the scene, the actor must use their Truth Brain to supply a natural and appropriate reason for this emphasis. Therefore, when announcing that they saw Miss Smith in the village on the day of the murder they must have a valid reason for doing so apart from the obvious need to supply the clue – in this case, the simple motivation of the character being genuinely suspicious of Miss Smith will suffice – provided the suspicion is logical to the character's knowledge of the situation in the first place.

The following points will enable you to ensure that everything you need to do technically when acting is executed truthfully:

- Is everything you do on stage rooted in proper motivation relevant to the scene, or are you saying and doing things purely because they have been directed or are in the script?

- Are you saying anything in the scene without knowing why?

- Are you moving in the scene without knowing why?

- Do you personally understand everything in the script including the lines of the other characters?

You must ensure that you have achieved understanding, motivation and truthful thought processes for everything that is required of you in the scene.

Example 4

An actor's memory fails a little and they are searching for the right word to say. The Truth Brain steps in and ensures that this appears as if the character is struggling to be articulate rather than that the actor has made a mistake. Good actors will do this instinctively. A similar situation applies when an actor has said the wrong word in error – the Truth Brain will have the character make the correction, not the actor.

THE TWO BRAINS IN PRACTICE

Now look carefully at the following words and learn them if possible:

> I've been thinking about us a lot recently and I've come to the conclusion that we should go our separate ways. It's over.

Give your Technical Brain the job of speaking this at least ten times, pausing before a different word each time. Upon each occasion allow your Truth Brain to provide a good and proper reason for the pause and see how naturalistic you can make it. Although you will, of course, never be required to do this when rehearsing a part, it makes an interesting way of testing your ability to remain natural whatever demands are made upon you technically.

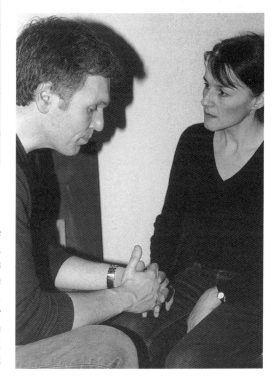

'I've been thinking about us a lot recently.'

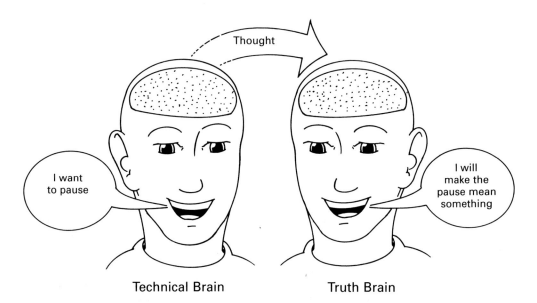

The Two-Brain Theory.

It is also important to understand that the Two-Brain Theory is simply a way of understanding a process and encouraging it to become instinctive. It is not necessary for you to think about it specifically when you are rehearsing or performing. As with all acting techniques, it is a means to an end – the end being 'truth'.

5 IMPROVISATION

ACTING *IS* IMPROVISATION

Improvisation is at the heart of everything an actor does. Far from being a sideline activity, an alternative way of working, it is a central mainstay – supporting and nurturing everything. It is true, of course, that improvisation has its own life, quite apart from the world of written drama in text form; improvised and devised theatre is a theatrical art form in itself and, as such, is worthy of much separate study. However, here you must concentrate upon the role of improvisation within acting generally, learning its significance in everything you do on stage and embracing it as an indispensable tool.

In a way, acting should always be improvised even when working with a script. You have already learnt that, even though an actor knows exactly what to say and where to move, the spontaneity of the performance is found in thinking and responding instinctively, as if each moment were a new and unrehearsed revelation. This is improvisation at work in its purest form – although an actor uses the playwright's words and actions, it is their 'improvisation' of thought and motivation, in real time on the stage, that brings the play alive.

Beyond this general and organic use of improvisation, it can also be used specifically in rehearsal as a device for informing and enhancing the actor's work. Improvising certainly brings the actor closer to reality and makes the job of finding truth easier, and working away from the text can greatly enhance the actor's abilities when they return to it. Before examining the various ways of employing improvisation fruitfully, there is a fundamental rule for improvising that must be learnt and taken to heart.

ACCEPT AND BUILD

Like acting itself, improvisation is a team game. Each individual will have their own ideas and agendas for the way in which any improvised work should develop, but it is imperative that they also take responsibility for embracing the input of others and moving the work forwards towards a mutually constructed outcome. Broadly, each actor should accept the contributions of others and build upon them. Consider the following bad example of effective improvising in an improvised exchange between two actors called John and Bill:

John: Hello, Bill.

Bill: Hello, John.

John: Did I see you in the park yesterday?

Bill: No.

Despite the simplicity of the example the lesson is clear – John is now completely stuck. Whatever John's idea of development may have been, Bill has stopped it full in its tracks, the improvisation has floundered after only four lines and thirteen words have been expended without any discernible dramatic achievement. Bill has not accepted what John has introduced into the improvisation and neither has he built upon it. The following alternative is not much better:

John: Hello, Bill.

Bill: Hello, John.

John: Did I see you in the park yesterday?

Bill: No. I went to the shops.

Bill has now at least made some kind of effort to move the improvisation forward, but has still completely ignored the contribution made by John, who will now have to reassert his park idea (thus being unproductively repetitive), or abandon it altogether in favour of Bill's lead. This is not supportive acting on Bill's part and, remembering that an actor is only as good as the actor they are working with, being supportive is a matter of self-preservation as well as courtesy. A far better way for Bill to respond would be this:

John: Hello, Bill.

Bill: Hello, John.

John: Did I see you in the park yesterday?

Bill: Yes. I just needed to get out of the house for a while.

OPPOSITE: **Improvisation will lead to freedom of expression.**

Bill has now accepted John's lead and built upon it. His own contribution has opened up possibilities for the scene in terms of discovering why he needed to escape his home, but is not too strong a dramatic idea to oust the possibility of exploring whatever John had in mind for the scene by introducing the topic of the park in the first place. By moving forwards in this way, they have the best chance of constructing a good scene from the best idea, both ideas in conjunction or, perhaps, a completely new idea that may yet develop.

However, a question need not necessarily be answered in the positive for it to be dramatically accepted and built upon. Consider this version of the four lines:

John: Hello, Bill.

Bill: Hello, John.

John: Did I see you in the park yesterday?

Bill: No! Why do you ask? Why do you think I was in the park? I wasn't anywhere near the park. I was at home all day. Ask my wife – she'll tell you.

There are now great possibilities for this scene to continue towards becoming an interesting and stimulating story as we discover why Bill is being so defensive about his whereabouts.

This rule of 'accept and build' also links to the necessity for all the actors taking part in an improvisation to be jointly responsible for moving the scene forward. Particularly when there are more than two participants involved, it is important that each individual contributes fully and imaginatively and does not 'sit on the sidelines', letting the others do all the work. On the other hand, it is equally important that they do not 'hog' the scene, allowing others to contribute and leave room for their ideas to be

Improvisation can be instructive and fun.

incorporated. Each actor must listen and think extremely actively and be totally engaged in the proceedings at all times. Again, these are exactly the same requirements as when working with a script.

LEARNING ABOUT THE CHARACTER

One of the most effective uses of improvisation within the rehearsal process is the exploration and development of the role you are playing. It is of course vital that all your characterizations are full and rounded, but this is not easy when they exist only in a selective series of scenes. In order to discover exactly how your characters think and to react in a truthful way, it is essential to explore their lives away from the

confines of the script. How you respond as a person in real life to any given situation is dependent upon your life and history as a whole and not just upon the stimulus of the present. So it is with the roles you play. The more you can explore the lives of these characters outside of the text, the more complete and whole they will appear when you are speaking their lines. You can achieve this by improvisation in both pedestrian and highly dramatic ways.

Imagine you are in a play in which your character has to fight successfully the symptoms of a severe illness. In order to get a 'feel' for the strength and resolve that your character must show, you (and your director) may decide to improvise certain character-building events in their past life; such as being bullied at school, coping with the early death of a parent, or convincing someone to employ them for a job to which they do not immediately appear suited.

On the other hand, a character does not only exist realistically in a play because of their dramatic strengths, but also because of the way they react as a human being generally. Therefore, it is equally valid to spend time improvising the more mundane aspects of their fictitious lives, such as making their breakfast in the morning; travelling to work in a crowded train; or having an argument in the bank about their overdraft. However, re-member that it is very rare to be involved in a rehearsal period that is not tight for time, so you should experiment with this type of improvisation alone and in your own time too.

LEARNING ABOUT THE DRAMA

Very often, a part that you are playing will be centred on a particular dramatic theme, which is of prime importance to the meaning and intentions of the play. If you are playing the lead role in a production you will probably be totally involved with this theme at many levels, but as a supporting character you are also likely to encounter it in most of the acting that you do.

If you return to the example of the person who is fighting an illness, you will see how this would be totally central to the performance of the leading character. However, were you to be playing a loved one of the hero (a parent or partner perhaps), you too would find your role totally focused towards the main thrust of the plot. If this were happening to you in life you would live through all of the situation chronologically: being worried about the symptoms; going to the doctor; waiting for the result of tests; telling your family; and so on. However, in a play some of these events may be missing; the story may start when you receive the test results, for instance, or, if you are playing a relative, when you are awaiting news from the operating theatre perhaps. In other words, the actor is often expected to have a full understanding of their character's situation without having experienced some of the most important moments of the crisis.

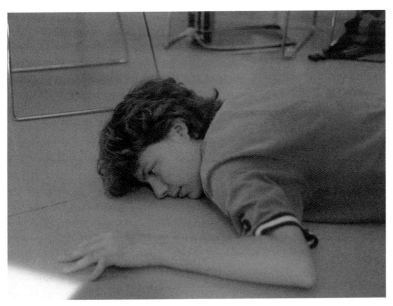

Improvisation helps an actor to explore the most dramatic of scenes.

This is where improvisation can be of invaluable help once again. By improvising these important scenes you will be able to gain a personal understanding and empathy with the situation you face on stage. For example, the play may not contain a scene where a doctor tells the character of their illness. This may be because the playwright did not feel that this was important within the overall shape of what they were trying to achieve in the play, or because they wished to keep the cast small and did not want to add another character (the doctor) for just one scene. However, the experience of this scene would be invaluable to an actor in placing their subsequent actions and reactions in context. Therefore, the scene may be improvised with the director or another actor playing the doctor and the lead actor given the chance to make real a very significant event in the story of their character.

An added luxury here is the option to play the scene in many different ways, experimenting perhaps with the varying reactions of the character to the news they are given. This methodology may also be applied to scenes that *do* exist within the play. Imagine that the scene between the hero and doctor actually is a part of the action and that it leads to a stoic acceptance by the patient, who then leaves the surgery holding back the tears. In the safety of the rehearsal room it is possible to try other reactions: perhaps they break down in front of the doctor; perhaps they become angry and refuse to accept what they are being told; or perhaps they adopt defensive tactics and greet the news with seeming indifference. Of course, none of these scenes is directly truthful to the play because they are not the version of events written, but, in allowing actors to explore other possibilities, it will enrich them with a greater understanding of how and why their character reacts as they do in the written scene.

IMPROVISING WHAT HAPPENED IN THE OTHER ROOM

Probably the most direct use improvisation can have in terms of supporting the text is in enabling the actor to know what has happened immediately before they enter a scene. You might have to arrive on stage from another room where you have been engaged in a furious argument with some unseen person. In reality, of course, you will be arriving cold,

An actor must know where he is coming from, as well as where he is going to.

having just made the journey from your dressing room – the last clue of the crossword still fresh in your mind. However, if you have improvised the argument in the rehearsal period you will be much better informed as to the state of mind to adopt as you walk on stage; the argument will no longer be totally imaginary as you will have actually experienced it.

This form of improvisation should not be taken to extremes: it is not necessary for you to improvise the scene in the wings each night before you go on. This would not only be pretentious but extremely distracting backstage. There is absolutely nothing wrong with still thinking about the crossword clue the second before you enter the stage, as long as you are fully informed as to how you should be acting immediately upon taking the stage. Improvisation is simply another tool in your box of acting aids.

It is not only the very immediate past that you need to be concerned with here. What happened in the next room may not, in fact, be as important as what happened that morning. The furious argument may have happened at the breakfast table; your character then travels to work and your first entry upon stage is as they enter their office. Not only may you still wish to improvise the argument as before, but also the journey to work – experimenting perhaps the character's thoughts and feelings as they sit on the train, thus knowing just how much they have or have not 'cooled down' as they walk upon the stage.

APPROACHING IMPROVISATION

There are two basic types of improvisation: those that are 'prepared' and those that are not. Any preparation may be as cursory or as thorough as you wish, but it will aim to set out certain criteria and methods of proceeding before the scene starts. For example, each

participant may be fully briefed as to the part they are to play, the development of the scene and what is to be achieved at each stage. This structuring may be determined by the director, the actors or everyone in conference, but the object of the exercise is to predetermine the basic shape and goals of the work prior to it starting. This approach is obviously often adopted when devising work, but is also a useful way of proceeding when exploring text in rehearsal. It can ingeniously combine the desirability to debate and discuss in the rehearsal room with the more practical benefit of linking this to performance, but in a 'safe area' away from the script.

The alternative is to improvise with no real attempt to prepare. The basic scenario will be stated (perhaps by the director) and the actors will then simply commence improvising and work through towards a conclusion. This works best if each attempt is followed by discussion and then the scene tried again – perhaps with a different priority or emphasis. This is an excellent way of proceeding if the object of the exercise is to explore as many ideas and angles of understanding as possible, but within a reasonably short time frame. This type of improvisation places a greater emphasis on the importance of the 'accept and build' rule, and cooperative improvising generally.

THE PARK BENCH

Examine the following exercise as an excellent example of simple improvising, suited to both a prepared and spontaneous approach:

Two chairs are placed side by side to form an imaginary park bench. Two actors are asked to sit on the bench playing the roles of people who are meeting there for the first time and quite by chance. They may be given no prior information at all – on the other hand, they may be given a variety of facts: who they are;

QUICK START GUIDE TO ACTING

8. Strict Improvising

Consider the following points carefully when improvising:

- Improvisations must progress forwards in a positive manner.
- Achieve positive progress by working as a team member, contributing to the development but not dominating.
- Unleash your imagination and banish inhibition. Have firm ideas about the improvisation and be brave enough to introduce them to the work.
- Be sensitive to the ideas of others – accept and build upon them.
- Attempt to incorporate the input of fellow actors with your own work, but only if you feel that this will be genuinely productive.
- If you feel that the improvisation is going wrong or becoming stale, take the initiative to stop it and regroup.

what they do for a living; what they must try to get from each other; what a particular outcome may be; a specific subject that they must introduce; or a combination of these and other factors. It is even possible to equip them with a full scenario of how the scene is to progress, and then allow them to conduct this towards a predetermined ending to the best of their abilities.

However this is used, it is one of the best ways to practise improvisation between two people. The bench can also be made bigger and other actors introduced to the scene if desired. If you can employ the help of a colleague, set up your bench and try this a few times, making sure to decide on any prerequisite facts before each attempt, and to agree to abide by the rule of accept and build. This will not only hone your improvising skills greatly but will be extremely enjoyable too.

Remember as you practise this (and any other improvisation) that the qualities of freedom, openness of mind, flexibility and willingness to take risks that you bring to the exercise are applicable to all of your acting.

6 MOVEMENT

THE ACTOR'S INSTRUMENTS

Most artists and craftspeople employ the tools of their trade, the instruments that enable them to practise their particular talents. These may be paintbrushes, cameras, potter's wheels or, in the case of musicians: violins, trumpets or pianos. The actor, too, requires the use of tools with which to work, or instruments upon which to play. However, these take a very different and unique form, because far from being outside objects acquired for their relevant purposes, the actor's instruments consist of his or her own body and voice.

However talented an actor may be, all expertise will come to nothing if the quality of the instruments is poor. True, a virtuoso violinist will get a reasonably impressive tune out of a cheap and battered violin, but it will take the likes of a Stradivarius in order for them to realize their full potential in the concert hall. Unfortunately for the actor, it is not possible to purchase a new body or voice however much money they may possess; their instruments are given to them at birth and so it is extremely important that these are developed and maintained properly. The tuning and fine-tuning of both the body and voice are essential if they are to provide good service and be at the actor's command for a lifetime.

The vocal instrument will be examined in the next chapter, but first it is vital to find a comprehensive appreciation of the instrument that not only contributes fulsomely to characterization and expression but literally carries you to the stage in the first place – the body. Mime has long been a theatrical discipline and, in recent times, there has been an increasing emphasis upon the body as a source of dramatic communication with the rise of 'Physical Theatre' and the theatre companies that have made it their expertise. Although this is in essence a specialist form of theatre, it connects absolutely to the way that the body must be used in acting generally and much can be learnt from watching drama being practised in this way. However, for your purposes you must initially take a slightly less demanding look at movement, with the aim of firmly establishing the fundamental principle for all drama, that the body must be a good and faithful servant to the actor's mind and enable communication rather than hinder it.

THE BODY BEAUTIFUL

Bodies come in all different shapes and sizes and, as theatre must aim to present as wide a view of life as possible, this is just as well. In the past, drama schools have vigorously encouraged their students to reduce weight and remain slim, but a more liberal view of body shape has developed over the years and diversity of physique is now seen as enriching, particularly with the development of television with its even greater need for realism. There is no doubt that you may want, for various reasons, to change the shape you are, but make sure that these reasons are good ones and not based upon a poor attitude to your own

appearance. It is very important that you accept and appreciate your body as part of the whole you, and this is dealt with in some detail in Chapter 8. However much you may want to alter your body image in the future, the body you have in the present is your sacred instrument and vital to your success as an actor. Likewise, the way you move and inhabit the space around you is uniquely part of 'you' and, as such, also of the characters you play.

The most important thing is to make sure that this instrument is working effectively and is fully geared to make you the best actor possible; that it expresses and moves freely and obediently to the intentions of your acting. This is not about perfection, nor is it about rejecting the body as an instrument because of any particular disability; it is about making sure that, whatever type of body and mobility you have, every part of you and every movement is appropriately honed for the job in hand. You must pay close attention to the things that will help to develop this tool and, perhaps more importantly, the things that will hinder it.

RELAXATION

There can be no doubt that one of the worst enemies of an actor is tension. It has already been established that acting is primarily concerned with utilizing the natural human communicating mechanism; this mechanism will not work if there is tension present. Physical tension is a blight in life generally, giving rise to all kinds of ailments; on stage it is equally disabling. It can impede the natural flow of your movement, stifle your ability to express your emotions and remove your ability to be naturally coordinated. In addition, physical tension will make its way swiftly to the voice and do equal amounts of damage there.

It is important to realize that not all tension is bad – it is muscle tension that enables us to stand up and walk about. However, unnecessary tension is a different matter, and it is vital for the actor to employ only the amounts of tension that are required for effective execution of any particular role. This can only be achieved by taking a long-term view of relaxation and making sure that the ability to relax becomes part of your daily life. There are varied ways to approach this, but the following exercise will make an excellent starting point. It should be practised regularly, but is particularly useful as part of your preparation for a performance or rehearsal.

Relaxation Exercise

- Remove your shoes and make sure that you are wearing loose, comfortable clothing. Lie on the floor with your head supported and raised from the ground by approximately eight centimetres – a large book is usually ideal for this. Let your arms lie by your side, slightly away from the body and with the palms turned upwards. Place your feet souls down upon the ground and draw them up towards your bottom so that your knees point upwards. Try to ensure that the whole of your spine is making contact with the floor and, likewise, your shoulders. Now close your eyes.
- Begin by taking long, slow breaths in through your nose and then slowly exhale through the mouth. Feel that every breath is taken deep down inside you and that it is long and slow. The object of this exercise is to relax but not to sleep, so imagine that with each inward breath you take in warm and revitalizing energy, and with each outward one you let go of and expel

OPPOSITE: An actor's movement must be released and free.

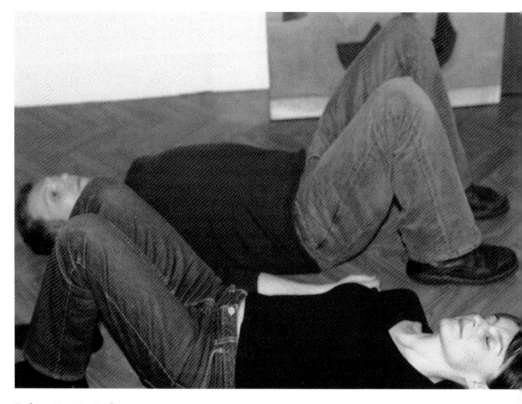

Relaxation is vital.

tension. Retain this focus upon your breathing throughout the exercise.

- Now imagine that you are lying on a sun-drenched, tropical beach. The sun is shining down upon you, filling you with comfort, warmth and energy. The only sound is the gentle lapping of waves.

- Starting with your toes, let your mind move slowly up along your body, consciously relaxing each body part as it goes. A useful mental aid to achieve this is to imagine that you are gradually filling up with lead and, as this happens, your body becomes heavier, sinking further into the imaginary sand beneath you.

- When this process is complete, remain relaxed upon the floor for about 15 minutes if possible, continuing to concentrate upon the depth and rhythm of your breathing. At the end of this time slowly sit and then stand up, and finally give yourself a gentle shake all over to feel fully revitalized.

RELAXATION OF THE MIND

Tension starts in the mind and therefore it is in the mind that the battle against it must begin. Always make sure that you are as mentally relaxed and focused as you can possibly be. Try to approach your life with acting as a major priority: you cannot act well if your mind is clogged with worries and problems, so resolve

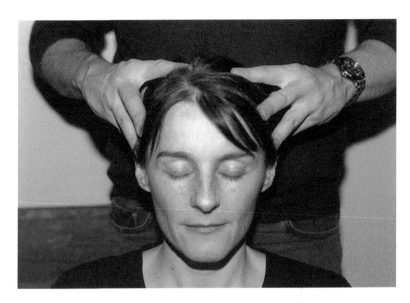

Actors may help each other to relax.

to deal with these as effectively as possible. Of course, there will be pressures and problems in your life that will be unavoidable (this is part of being human and provides the raw material that the actor uses), but make sure that you face up to problems and don't let anything fester in your mind.

In the same way, it is important to remain mentally relaxed when you are rehearsing or performing. Inevitably there will be times when things are going badly, nothing you try will work and you will feel bogged down in your own inadequacy – unfortunately this is part of being an actor. When this happens be proactive in finding a solution. If you have a bad day at rehearsals, make sure you get clear in your mind the nature of the problem and speak to the director the very next morning with the express intention of finding a solution. Do not let anything get out of proportion and stay positive in your approach to everything you do. Be especially carefully not to allow interpersonal issues between you and other members of the company to get out of hand. It is very difficult to concentrate on your acting if

there are other unrelated agendas that are unresolved amongst your fellows. Anything that stops you concentrating fully on stage must be eliminated as much as is humanly possible. Not being able to concentrate properly on stage will eventually lead you to feel it to be an alien world and one in which you are not at home – this must be avoided at all costs.

LIMBERING AND COORDINATION

As well as a relaxed body it is also essential that an actor has a well-limbered one. Actors do not need to be athletes, but they do need to be toned and loose in order to move effectively on stage. They must also be well coordinated, with movement that flows naturally and obediently from thought and intention. However talented you may be, if you are physically blocked and unresponsive you will not be able to act to anywhere near your full potential.

In order to promote good movement, you must live a life that has physical activity as a priority – generally speaking, 'couch potatoes' make poor actors. For this reason you should regularly practise at least one sport of your choice. It does not really matter what this is (the important thing is to get out there and 'move', but some sports lend themselves to the actor's art better than others. For instance, sport that builds muscle tone is not nearly as useful as one that promotes coordination and stamina. Therefore, tennis is generally a better choice than weight lifting. However, any activity is better than none, and even if you only manage a brisk walk several times a week,

you will at least be making movement part of your routine. Swimming is also excellent exercise for your purposes.

Many people underestimate the need for physical fitness. Do not make this mistake, as acting requires great stamina and control.

It is also imperative that you keep your body stretched and loose. Therefore, along with your regular attention to relaxation, you should also practise a frequent limber routine. It is impossible to overstress the importance of this, and the actor who neglects this side of their craft is not truly serious about it. You would not expect a violin to play properly if it were left in a cupboard and not maintained; neither can you expect your body to work as your loyal and responsive instrument if you do not keep it tuned and toned.

There are many ways that you can achieve this state of limber. If you wish to be communal about it, joining a regular dance class will be ideal. Dance will stretch you both mentally and physically, and teach you coordination, stamina and control. However, if this is not for you, aim to have a limber routine of your own that you can do on a reasonably regular basis. There are many exercises that this routine can contain (you should aim to vary it anyway), but the important thing is to stretch and limber each part of the body and keep yourself supple as a whole.

There is obviously an age factor to take into account here and younger people will be able to be more ambitious in their programme than those of more mature years. Those with disabilities will also need to be selective, but everyone should be able to keep limbered to an appropriate degree.

As a starting point, use the following routine regularly as a means of keeping supple and to achieve a degree of physical release. As with the relaxation exercise, it will be particularly useful before you start working and should be used in conjunction with relaxation techniques. It will also help to develop a strong, straight (but not ridged) posture; this is vital for the actor. Read through it completely before you start so that you are aware of all the instructions.

A Basic Limber Routine

- Stand with your feet about shoulder width apart, flex your knees a little, tuck your bottom under, relax your shoulders and lengthen your neck by making sure that your head is level with the chin and not pointing too high. You should feel that the majority of tension in your body is confined to the lower half (making you strong and giving you a solid contact with the ground), with the area above the belt line floating free and relaxed. Particularly ensure that the shoulders and neck are free of all unnecessary tension.
- Begin by raising one hand to waist height and shaking it from the wrist. Try to keep the arm as still as possible at first and keep the fingers relaxed.
- Now let the shaking movement travel into the arm, keeping the elbow flexed and the shoulder relaxed.
- Keep this movement going as you repeat the process with your other hand and arm.
- Gradually let the movement subside and return your hands to hang loosely by your sides.

- Making sure that you remain in balance, raise one foot off the ground and slowly rotate it in a clockwise direction from the ankle.
- After ten turns, reverse the direction for a further ten.
- Now gently shake the foot and gradually let this shaking extend into your whole leg. Keep it gentle and relaxed, trying to retain a good balance on your opposite leg at all times.

- Return your foot to the ground and repeat with your other foot.
- Return to the posture as before.

- Drop your head down so that your chin rests upon your chest, but do not let the shoulders fall forwards as you do this.
- Gently roll your head to the right so that your right ear moves towards your right shoulder. You should feel a gentle stretch but don't force it.
- Now let your head roll back down and continue across to the other side.
- Continue this movement back and forth and gradually increase the momentum. Imagine that your head is filled with something that is very heavy and that it is being swung back and forth on the end of your neck. Keep the neck very relaxed and keep the movement very free and easy.
- When you feel that you have enough momentum, let the head continue up and around to the right, maintaining now a circular movement. However, do not let the head fall too far back at the top of the circle, as this puts too much strain upon the neck and can be dangerous.
- After ten repetitions of this circle, let your chin come to rest again on your chest and now repeat the whole pattern again, this time letting the circle begin towards the left and thus make the circle follow the opposite direction for another ten repetitions.
- Bring your head to rest with your chin again upon your chest. Now clasp your hands together and simply place them upon the back of your neck. Do not push, but just let the natural weight of your hands give your neck a gentle extra stretch.
- Loosen the neck again with a few small circles and then gently raise it to a normal upright position.
- Now begin to rotate the shoulders slowly in a backwards direction, while making

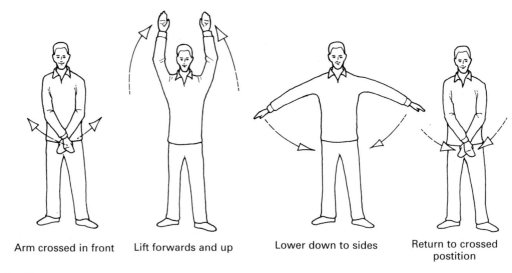

Arm crossed in front   Lift forwards and up   Lower down to sides   Return to crossed postition

Circling arms.

sure that they travel as big a route as possible – let them go high towards the ears, then right back and down, and then far forwards and up to complete the circle.

- As you do this, occasionally let the head bob and turn just a little to ensure that the neck remains relaxed.
- After ten slow repetitions, reverse the direction for another ten.
- Let your shoulders come to rest and now place your hands behind your back with your fingers clasped and your thumbs together. Pull gently down with the hands, but make sure that the back remains straight. This will give a little extra stretch to your shoulders. Push down and release several times, but keep the stretch gentle and don't overdo it.
- Return to your normal posture.

- Starting with your arms by your side, move your hands to cross in front of you and then lift them up in front of you and stretch them towards the ceiling. As you do this, keep your arms straight but don't raise your shoulders any more than is necessary.

- Uncross your hands and push them outwards as you let them slowly descend to each side of you, forming a 'cross' position as they are halfway down. Keep the arms stretched and maintain a steady control in the descent.
- Let your hands cross in front of you again and continue this circular movement for ten repetitions.
- Gently roll the neck and shoulders again a little to ease out any tension.
- Keeping the bottom half of your body firm, let your chest collapse into a concave shape, but retaining the head looking forwards.
- Now correct this, letting your chest come up and forwards and your shoulders back. Do not push the chest out, as if you were in the army, but rather feel open across the shoulders with your chest just leading forwards. Your head should continue to float freely on your neck.
- Repeat this collapsing and straightening

Stretching and limbering is the key to an expressive body.

Letting everything 'hang'.

for twenty repetitions, trying to achieve a muscle memory of a good upright posture as it is achieved each time.

- Widen your stance to approximately double shoulder width, but ensure that you still feel firmly planted on the ground.
- Let your head drop forward again, only this time continue the momentum downward, letting your shoulders follow the head; your back curves and your hands fall forward and down towards the floor. Keep your knees flexed at this stage, allowing your fingers to touch the floor with ease. Relax your neck totally so that your head droops and hangs free; at the bottom your view should be between your legs.

- Once in this position, gently swing from side to side, trailing your hands along the floor to reach each foot in turn. Maintain a feeling of 'hanging' in this position with very little tension in the top half of your body.
- Return your hands to the centre and begin a very gentle bounce, letting the palms of your hands touch the floor at the bottom of each bounce. Throughout this, keep the knees slightly bent. These bounces should only be gentle and small – you should not be bouncing towards being upright again.
- Move the bounce from side to side, visiting each foot again in turn. Maintain a feeling of being a very limp rag doll and keep the

neck totally 'switched off'. Bounce to each foot ten times.

- Repeat this, but now as you bounce towards each foot, straighten the other leg. You will feel a good stretch in the straightened leg as you do this. Again, make twenty repetitions in all. If you find this difficult, only touch fingers upon the floor and not palms.
- Return to the central position and bounce a further five times.
- Straighten both legs and bounce five times again. You may find that you can only touch your fingertips to the ground while your legs are straight. If even this is difficult, let your hands hang as close to the ground as possible; you will find that each time you do this exercise you will be able to get closer to the ground, but, whatever you do, don't force it.
- Complete thirty bounces in all this way, alternating between five with knees bent and five with legs straight.
- Return to hang in the central position and then very slowly curl up the spine to an upright position again, ensuring that the head is the last part of your body to come up straight in an exact reverse of the downwards journey.
- Shake the whole body gently to loosen everything up again.

- Now sit on the floor with your legs straight and open to no more than about 45 degrees (and less if this is more comfortable). Flex your feet so that your toes point upwards and the flat of your foot faces forwards. Keep your back straight and your head level as before.
- Leading with the chest and maintaining the straight back, push forwards and return for ten repetitions. You will feel a good stretch in your legs and lower back as you do this.

Quick Start Guide to Acting

10. Physical Response

Never underestimate the importance of attaining a body that is loose and supple. When you are acting properly your mind will be sending a multitude of signals, just as it does in life. It will expect the body to respond just as readily and naturally, even though the demands may far exceed those of daily living.

Do not forget that not only will you be trying to portray a character that might be quite different from yourself, in a fictitious situation that may be highly emotional and dramatic, but you will have the added pressure of an audience watching and judging your every move. Under these circumstances, your normal ability to remain physically coordinated and expressive may break down, unless you have given sufficient attention to maintaining a fit, healthy and limbered readiness.

- Now bend the back and lower your head to look at the floor. Push forwards a further ten times, but now leading with the hands to touch the floor as far in front of you as possible without too much discomfort.
- Straighten your back again and lift your head. Turn your torso towards your right foot and push forwards with the chest again ten times.
- Repeat with back bent and arms forwards as before.
- Repeat the same process towards your left foot and then in the centre again.
- Repeat this circuit three times in all.
- Stand up and have a good but gentle shake of the whole body to finish.

This routine is, of course, very basic and should be developed and varied. However, always seek expert advice about your movement work and consult your doctor if you have any doubts at all about your physical regime. The important thing is to keep moving and to consider quality of movement to be an essential part of your existence.

THE IMPORTANCE OF BEING CENTRED

A most important part of an actor's physicality is centring. This simply means that everything that the actor does, physically, vocally and even spiritually must originate from the centre. This does not just mean the centre of the actor's body, but the centre of the actor's soul too.

Because acting starts in the head, it is very easy for the 'centre' to be pulled up high towards it; too much expression happens in the upper part of the body, especially the shoulders, neck and head, and the rest of the body gets forgotten. The result is a kind of physical and emotional 'top heaviness', with gestures emanating high in the body and seeming jerky and incomplete. It is this lack of centre that can make an actor look awkward and uncoordinated on stage, and can lead to a shallowness of movement, speech and expression.

Closely connected to centring is weight placement. An actor's weight should sink

Actors must have their 'weight down' and a strong 'centre'.

downwards towards the ground. Make sure when you are working that your centre of gravity is not too high, that you feel well connected to Mother Earth at all times and that the majority of your bodily tension remains in your bottom half. Focus upon your Centre and feel that everything – voice, movement and emotion – emanates from there. Again, sport (especially ball games) will be of invaluable help in this.

7 VOICE

THE VOICE BEAUTIFUL

Your voice is an instrument that requires just as much careful maintenance and fine-tuning as your body; perhaps more so, if it is to become a willing and pliant servant to your acting abilities.

The first thing you must do is to banish all of the negative feelings that you may have developed about your voice during your life. Many people feel desperately insecure about their voice and, if this applies to you, then remedial action must be taken straight away. There are two main reasons for this insecurity. Firstly, because humans never hear their own voices accurately, as others hear them, they find it difficult to trust the sound they are making and rarely like or appreciate the uniqueness of their personal sound. Secondly, the human mind subconsciously realizes that the voice is a major reflection of personality, and therefore it becomes an obvious target for inhibition and stress.

OPPOSITE: *A powerful and resonant voice requires expansion of the torso.*

Because all of this is simply a state of mind, it is infinitely curable by fostering a new way of thinking about your voice. Think of your voice work not as a means to recreate or even improve your voice, but as a way of enhancing, liberating and promoting the beauty, flexibility and individuality that it already contains. Nobody has a bad voice, but many people have voices that need to be freed from the constraints of self-doubt and under-utilization.

You must begin by laying to rest those old childhood memories of being told only to 'speak when you are spoken to' and the taunts of 'liking the sound of your own voice'. As you progress with your acting skills now is the time to have faith in the sound you make, find confidence in the words you speak and be proud of the voice that is uniquely yours. You must start to make full and proper use of this magnificent gift; it will not work for the characters you play if it is not encouraged to work for you. Envisage your voice as something that will win you friends, influence colleagues and entertain your audience.

As with so much of acting, voice work is primarily about having the right attitude – having started to adopt this attitude you are ready to begin looking at the various aspects of voice upon which you can work.

Projection and Power

Projection is not just a matter of voice. As an actor you will also need to be concerned with the projection of energy and thought – both of which require far more than just vocal skill. Neither is projection simply about volume and clarity of speech. Clarity of mind and purpose is just as important. However, these will be dealt with later, and voice shall be your prime concern here.

In the same way that it is important not to think of projection only in terms of volume, so it is important not to think of volume solely in terms of raising your voice or shouting. This may seem obvious, but it is surprising how many inexperienced actors achieve what they think is projection in this way.

In life, most people talk at a volume level that is suitable to reach the ears of other people who are standing reasonably near to them. If they need to communicate with someone who is a good distance away they shout – like shouting across the street or a crowded room. Volume levels in between these two extremes are rarely needed and, if they are, it is at this level that humans will be least confident about the quality of their sound and its effectiveness. However, actors constantly need to employ many different volume levels and very often in a quite artificial way. The scene they are playing may require them to talk to another character who is quite close in the same room, but in order to project this to the back of the auditorium they must use more volume than usual, while continuing to make it sound natural.

The 'petrol' that drives the 'engine' of the voice – its volume and power – is breath. The actor needs to develop skill levels of deep breathing and control of breath that are not particularly important in daily life. The limited demands that life makes upon breathing from a vocal point of view mean that humans tend to breath quite shallowly; the major purpose of breathing remains the continuance of life and provided air is moving in and out of the body, all is well. Neither is control of breath a vital factor. The body breathes out and takes another breath when required – regardless of the fact that process of speaking may be occurring. Clarity of speech and continuity of communication are rarely seen as vital. This is undoubtedly a shame: as technological communication becomes more and more prevalent in our society, so personal communication seems to decline. However, regrettable as this may be it is not your immediate concern as an actor. What *is* your concern, however, is the complete reversal of these standards when on stage and acting.

Both the depth of the inward breath and your ability to control the outward breath in terms of speaking is of prime importance. Clarity is imperative, and a voice that falls away at the end of a sentence or phrase because all of the breath has been expended too quickly can be disastrous. Neither does the actor have the luxury of breathing exactly when they want. The demands of the text, or indeed the intentions of the character, may require breathing at the end of long phrases and not in the middle of them; this is, of course, particularly relevant when speaking verse – perhaps Shakespearian.

It will be helpful at this stage to look at depth of breath and control separately.

Deep Breathing

As an experiment, place one hand upon your stomach and the other on the lower rear part of your ribcage. Expel your breath and push until you are quite empty and then hold for a few seconds. As you begin to feel un-comfortable relax and allow your body to breathe in deeply. Because you have really forced your existing breath out and then deprived yourself of a further breath for a short while, your brain will get the message that it needs to instruct your body to breathe fully and deeply. You should also feel with your hands an expansion of both the ribs and the stomach. This is caused by your ribcage acting like bellows and expanding to draw breath into the body, and your diaphragm dropping down and, by the nature of your physiology, displacing your stomach in a forwards direction. Now just slowly breathe out again and repeat several times.

It is important to feel the amount of expansion in your body as you take these deep breaths. It is often thought that an intake of breath somehow makes you small – as when you are told to 'breathe in' when entering a crowded lift for instance. This is totally the wrong image. Breathing makes you bigger and, as you practise this deep-breathing technique, concentrate on getting bigger, stronger and ready to fill the world with your sound.

Another misconception about breathing is that the shoulders should be raised to aid a large inhalation. This finds its origins in the subconscious knowledge that the ribs play a large part in the process – which, of course, they do. However, the ribcage does not move in this way (as you can feel with your hand) and the shoulders should remain still and level; to raise them artificially will create tension. Unnecessary tension in any part of the body should be avoided, but it is particularly undesirable in the upper parts, where it will quickly affect the voice and lead to a harsh, strained sound.

Make sure that every inward breath you take is through your nose rather than the mouth. This will prevent your mouth from becoming dry – a very important factor, especially when playing a long part with many lines to say.

When you practise deep breathing try to fix a mental image in your mind of filling with breath from the bottom of your torso upwards.

Although this has no basis in biology, it will subconsciously promote free and expansive movement of the breathing apparatus. A useful, but slightly unsavoury image, is to pretend that the inward breath is taken through the bottom rather than the head.

When you have experienced this sensation of deep breathing, try to practise it regularly and employ it in your day-to-day life. The ideal is to retrain your body to work in this way quite naturally without you having to think about it consciously. Not only will this improve the volume and clarity of your voice, but it will also begin to sound fuller and more resonant. Imagine yourself as a very expensive high-fidelity sound system – a more powerful amplifier not only leads to greater levels of sound but far greater quality of sound too.

CONTROL OF BREATH

Now that you have started to breathe deeply you must begin to experiment with controlling the outward breath. Try breathing out on an 's' sound (like the sound of escaping gas) over a silent count of approximately fifteen seconds. It is more than possible that your first attempt will end in failure and you will either completely run out of breath early or be really straining towards the end. This is because too much air will spill out at the start of the sound. Try again and consciously control the breath from the beginning. Concentrate on pulling up the diaphragm (this feels like pulling in your stomach) and slowly letting the ribs subside from their expanded position after the inward breath. Feel that the throat is open – control is gained from the correct use of ribs and diaphragm, not by 'closing down' on the sound and inhibiting it.

Try to keep the 's' sound steady throughout the count. If you find this difficult reduce the count to ten, or even five, and then slowly build back up to fifteen and on to twenty if possible.

'Ah' – an open throat and jaw allow the voice to flow out.

the first two counts into an 'ah' sound (the sound in the word 'car'), and then complete the count. 'Ah' is the most open of the vowel sounds, with jaw fully open, tongue flat in the mouth and lips totally relaxed and inactive. With the throat open (as it should be) there is plenty of room for the sound to tumble out in an uncontrolled manner, so keep tabs on your ribs and diaphragm and make sure they work smoothly and precisely in order to deliver the sound steadily. Remember to keep the sound 'forward' – relax and enjoy the experience of your voice flowing freely out of you.

Try doing this with as many sounds as possible ('ooh' as in 'do', 'ee' as in 'tea' and 'er' as in 'her' are some good examples), and concentrate on achieving a relaxed but powerful and controlled sound. Above all, enjoy the sound of your voice: if you do not like your sound, you cannot expect an audience to. If any of this makes you feel giddy or hyperventilated, stop at once.

POWER AND CONTROL IN PRACTICE

The object of the exercise here is control in every sense – you should not try to finish the count with breath left over, but be just about empty as the count is complete. Push firmly on the 's' sound and trust your breathing apparatus to work properly for you; it will happily do this once it has been educated as to your expectations of it.

When you can do this easily, replace the 's' with a 'hum' on any comfortable note. Concentrate on keeping the sound steady again but, in addition, keep the sound forward on the lips – producing a mild tingling sensation – and at all times avoiding the sound dropping back into the throat. When you feel confident with this, let the jaw drop open after

Once you have extended your breathing and mastered its control in this way, you will be able to apply it to the speaking of text. Being able to breathe when you want to, rather than when you run out of breath, is extremely liberating and allows you to concentrate on the important task of interpretation. The feeling of security that you will develop will enable you to be totally flexible in your changes of volume, pitch and pace, and allow you often to simply 'top up' your breath when it is convenient to do so. Speak the following lines of Shakespeare, breathing only where indicated, and trying to let the voice flow freely and colourfully from you. Use as many different notes in your voice as you can and swell and decrease the volume at will:

Shall I compare thee to a summer's day? (*Breath*)
Thou art more lovely and more temperate. (*Breath*)
Rough winds do shake the darling buds of May, (*Breath*)
And summer's lease hath all too short a date. (*Breath*)

Now repeat this, but try to use only one breath for the third and fourth lines. Then try this more difficult example:

O for a Muse of fire, that would ascend
The brightest heaven of invention, (*Breath*)
A kingdom for a stage, princes to act
And monarchs to behold the swelling scene! (*Breath*)

Then should the warlike Harry, like himself,
Assume the port of Mars; (*Breath*) and at his heels,
Leash'd in like hounds, should famine,
Sword and fire, (*Breath*)
Crouch for employment.

This is the opening speech from Shakespeare's *King Henry V*, and is an enthusiastic address to the audience by a narrator. Use the power and colour of your voice to create an exciting and vibrant atmosphere. The breath before the final line should be used in a way so as not to break the sense of the ongoing phrase but to give energetic emphasis to the last three words. Speak these words when you are alone in the house and, free from all inhibition, really let your voice have its wings and enjoy yourself.

'O for a Muse of fire.'

When using volume, make sure that there is no feeling of strain in your throat and that all the power comes from breath and your skilful use of it.

As well as power and control, the actor must give thought to the quality of voice produced. It has already been established that your voice will possess its own particularly special sound, but now is the time to develop and enjoy its richness. A pleasant-sounding and emotionally pliable voice is achieved by obtaining a full and resonant sound, and this is very much about finding and cultivating what is already there, rather than constructing a new voice that is technically impossible. It should be the actor's aim to foster the best degree of resonation possible for their own particular vocal capabilities.

It is true that some people are born with richer, more resonantly satisfying voices than others, but do not waste your time wishing for another's voice – take pride in your own and make sure that you utilize its capabilities and beauty to the full. One of the most common mistakes, particularly amongst male actors, is to try to make the voice sound more resonant by forcing the voice down into a lower pitch, which actually has the opposite effect. Although it is desirable to extend the pitch of your voice, trying to speak at a lower register will generally tighten the voice and inhibit resonation rather than release it. Always let the voice work from a middle note that is comfortable for you (even if you feel this is too high) and place the voice forward in your mouth, rather than try to let it rumble in your chest. In doing this, you will paradoxically allow the voice to resonate far more freely at all levels.

RELAX THE JAW

There are three primary places where the voice resonates. These are the mouth, the pharynx and (for some sounds) the nose. Other places in the body provide secondary resonation, particularly the head and chest. If you decide to take your study of voice further you will need to explore these in detail, but for your purposes here it will be sufficient to concentrate upon the mouth, as all resonation is linked to using it correctly.

Basically, it is essential to allow as much space as possible within the mouth for the sound to resonate. Think for a moment of a stringed musical instrument such as a guitar, violin or double bass. While the sound emerges from the hole in the body of the instrument, it resonates within the body itself. Think of the gap between your lips and teeth as the exit hole for the sound, but remember that it is inside the 'cave' of the mouth that the resonation happens. If you were to stuff newspaper into the hole of your guitar you would reduce the resonation space and spoil the sound. Therefore, if you reduce the space within your mouth you will do likewise.

It is easier said than done to allow the necessary space within the mouth. In the course of speaking, the mouth and all its associated parts move a great deal: the lips push forwards and back; the back of the tongue rises up and down; the tip of the tongue moves this way and that; and the jaw opens and closes. All of this activity is for the complex objective of creating the vowel sounds and consonants that make up words. However, the key player in this whole process is the jaw.

The jaw tends to be too tight and not to release open enough. This is for two basic reasons: firstly, by erring towards a more closed position the jaw makes the job of the tongue and lips much easier by keeping the area within which they have to move and stretch comparatively small; secondly, modern-day stress and tension find no better resting place than in the jaw, and this tension inhibits full and free motion. In general, the jaw should maintain a constant opening of the mouth measuring roughly the width of

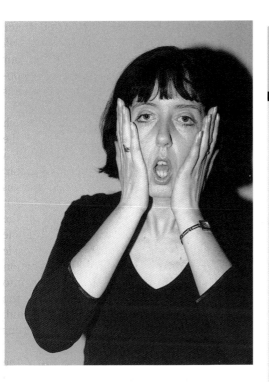

A relaxed jaw is of prime importance.

your first two fingers held on top of one another. Of course, this will change a little as you speak, but it is the ideal that the jaw should always be returning to this amount of separation.

This can only be achieved by relaxing the jaw rather than by forcing it open. The naturally inert position of the jaw is in fact open – it is muscle movement that closes the jaw. When asleep (or dead) the jaw tends to 'drop' open naturally and you must try to develop the same response when speaking. Try to let the tongue and lips do most of the work and keep the jaw as relaxed as possible at all times. It must remain flexible and it will move, but try always to gravitate towards the open position and match this with a good open feeling in your throat too: give your sound as much opportunity as possible to emerge from you free and uninhibited.

Relax your jaw by stroking it down with your hands on both sides of your face and letting it hang naturally – in a 'gormless' attitude.

RESONATION IN PRACTICE

Sing again the 'ah' (car) sound on one single, comfortable note, remembering to start with a hum (to push the voice forward and avoid a glottal shock as you start) and then letting the jaw drop open. Really feel that your jaw is as relaxed and open as possible. Allow gravity to do its work, then you should glorify in the large space within your mouth and the wide-open passage from which the sound comes up and out. A helpful image here is that of a ventriloquist's dummy – its jaw is arranged to drop straight down, rather than being hinged to 'open and close'. This will help you to visualize the process of relaxation and openness.

Now try singing the sound 'ooh' (do); there is no need to hum first now as the 'd' will push the voice forward naturally. With this sound the lips are pushed forward and therefore the opening of the mouth is quite small (probably not much more than pencil width). However, the resonating area behind the opening and within the mouth must remain as large as possible and this will be achieved by keeping the jaw relaxed. By doing this you will achieve a resonantly pleasant sound to the 'ooh' rather than a thin and restricted one. Experiment by relaxing and closing the jaw as you sing the 'ooh' but retaining a constant position of the lips pushed forward – you should hear the difference quite dramatically.

Return to the Shakespearian verses and speak them again, now concentrating upon keeping a relaxed jaw and a free and pleasant sound. Feel that every part of you is contributing to the generation of the sound and that there is absolutely nothing to stop it travelling out and away from you. Think of your voice as a child that you conceive and nurture, and then watch with pride as it gains independence, strength and freedom.

RECEIVED PRONUNCIATION

It has already been made clear that having confidence in your voice is a major factor in enabling it to be used an effective tool. Part of this confidence must lie in an acceptance of the particular native accent that you have. The wealth of the various sounds that stem from different areas both nationally and internationally is one of the great joys of the human voice and should be embraced as such. Never be ashamed of your own way of speaking, but rather take pride in its individuality and colour.

However, it is generally considered that actors may require a neutral standard of speech in order to be able to move away from this central core towards assuming other accents and speech patterns. It is also a requisite for speaking much (although certainly not all) of the classical repertoire of literature. This can be a contentious issue and 'Received Pronunciation' (or 'Standard English' as it used to be known) is certainly less of a prerequisite for acting than it was in the past. It is something that you should bear in mind, although the acquiring of it is a study in itself and will involve you in more work than is required here.

For the present, be content to concentrate upon the clarity of your speech and the openness of the sounds you make. Aim for a full and rounded sound and try not to emphasize any particular regional traits when practising voice. Find your own version of a neutral voice: one that is complete in its resonance but also unaffected, and is ready to move effectively towards the sound required for the characters you play.

BE PRECISE

Sloppy and lazy diction has, in many instances, become an accepted feature of much regional speech. However, the actor must avoid this type of inaccuracy at all costs. True, some of the characters you play may not require accuracy of diction, but many others will and you must be able to achieve sharp and precise diction at will and quite naturally.

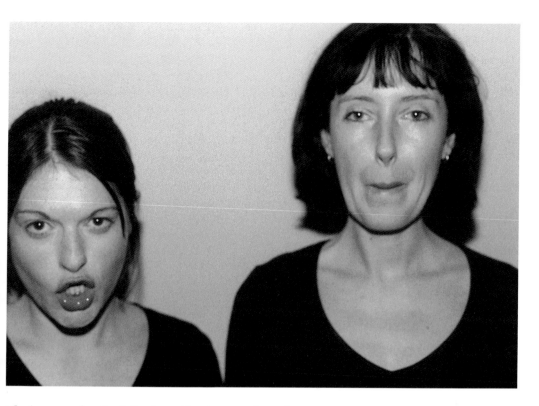

The 'organs of articulation' must be strong and precise.

Diction is a subject in itself and it is not necessary for you to delve into its complexities here. However, there are some simple imperatives that can be identified and practised:

- Make sure that all of your consonants are clear and sharp. Don't be overemphatic with them, but do keep them crisp and precise and, above all, evident. Consonants may be missed altogether if you are not careful (particularly at the ends of words), so do make sure that they are given the attention they deserve – they are, after all, the very skeleton of the words you speak. You may be fleshing out this skeleton with beautifully resonate vowel sounds, but, if the 'bones' are missing, all will collapse.

Most poor diction can be cured by strengthening of the tongue and lips and a little drilling to get them to make each consonant correctly in the mouth.

The Lips

In order to strengthen the lips try the following:

- Relax the jaw and then push the lips as far forward as they will go as if planting a full kiss on someone's face. Now pull them back into a purse, as if you have just tasted a bitter lemon. Really make them stretch and give them a good work-out. Repeat until they ache just a little, then blow through them, as a horse would do, to relax them again.

- Now alternate the speaking of these words, making sure that all the 'p' and 'b' consonants are sounded clearly with a light but precise movement of the lips coming together and then parting cleanly. Give equal attention to the first and last letter of each word and don't forget to keep the jaw relaxed throughout:

  - pup
  - pub
  - bap
  - bop
  - pap
  - pop
  - pip.

- Repeat the list several times, increasing the speed of speaking each time but maintaining precision.
- Now speak the following sentence with equal definition of 'p' and 'b' and, again, increase the speed on each attempt. As you do this, pay attention to the clarity of all the other consonants and sounds too:

  - A piece of paper is by far the better place for placing proper pencil marks with big beautiful loops and pretty dappled dabs of bonny baby scribbles.

The Tongue

The tongue particularly needs strength in order to do its job properly and to achieve this it must be worked just like any other muscle:

- Drop your jaw open as far as it will comfortably go and then stretch the tip of the tongue to touch the roof of the mouth, then to the bottom, then to the right and left sides – pushing the cheeks out hard, and really stretching the tongue. Finally, stick the tongue out of the mouth as far as

it will go, turning up the tip as you do so. Really stretch the tongue and continue this 'round' until it begins to ache a little and then stop.

- The following words and sentences can then be worked as before. Keep 't' and 's' sounds sharp, making them with the tongue tip behind the upper teeth and not letting too much air escape. Push the tongue tip between the teeth for the 'th' sounds, especially at the end of words where it is very often neglected and replaced by an 'f':

  - tan
  - top
  - tip
  - tap

  - sip
  - sap
  - sup
  - sun

  - thin
  - than
  - think
  - thick

  - bath
  - worth
  - moth
  - maths.

  - The thin man sat on the thick tin trestle and thought through his sad thoughts in a singularly sentimental, transcendental type of thinking.

  - Two taps sitting on the bath is best in terms of soaking showers and tremendously tiring times trickling tributaries of wet water.

MORE VOICE WORK

By following the suggestions of this chapter you will come to understand and appreciate your voice, and be able to keep it sufficiently tuned and responsive. However, this is a subject that you can, and should, pursue further. Working on your voice as an actor is not an option but a necessity. As you grow in confidence you should examine and correct any defects in your vocal technique, and make sure that all of the idiosyncrasies that make your speech part of the unique 'you' are fully under your control when playing characters who would speak differently. Enjoy your voice work and your voice.

8 CHARACTERIZATION

WORKING WITH YOURSELF

In order to approach characterization correctly you must recognize from the outset that you cannot become another person; you can only bring another person to life through you. It is not possible to walk into your dressing room before a performance, hang yourself up upon one of the pegs and take down your character to 'put on'. You only have yourself to work with and, therefore, you must see characterization not as an exercise in creating a new personality but as a rearranging and reprioritizing of your own.

If you examine any of the great character actors you will notice two very important things. Firstly, they are able to portray a varied range of different characters, but secondly (and more importantly), each portrayal contains a large measure of their own 'self'; their own unique 'being'. Although these factors may seem contradictory, they are not. The skill of acting is to use yourself in such a way as to allow the role you are playing to emerge from deep within you, not to wear it like a coat. There will be times when this process renders you completely unrecognizable, but this will not happen every time, and it is not a prerequisite to truthful characterization.

OPPOSITE: **Characterization must permeate the body and voice, even when in repose.**

In order to be a good actor, far from 'loosing yourself' in the character, you must 'find' the character in you.

Because of this, it is vital that you pay close attention to your two basic instruments (voice and body) and keep them well maintained. Reaffirm in your mind the importance of strength, coordination, relaxation and flexibility. These qualities will never be more important to you than when you are trying to draw a truthful and realistic character from yourself. You need to be able to take them for granted so that you can concentrate on the important mental processes involved. One of the most important factors to consider is the understanding and development of yourself.

KNOWING YOU

Before you can hope to play a range of emotionally complex and diverse characters, all of which must spring from you and only you, you must have a rounded concept of who you are as a person and feel comfortable with yourself. You cannot expect to acquire a personal knowledge and understanding of the fictitious characters you play until you have acquired a similar knowledge and understanding about the 'real' you.

This must be approached in two ways – externally and internally. You need an insight into the way the world looks at you in physical terms (the way you move and talk), and an equal insight into your inner soul: you need to have a concept of what makes you 'tick'; what

Good characterization lies in mind, body and voice – not just costume and make-up.

you do and don't like (and why); your personal priorities in life; and the various qualities that make the unique 'you'.

But, most importantly, you need to be able to accept, understand and be at one with yourself – you need to feel comfortable in your own skin. It is not necessary to like yourself (although this would help), or to feel positive about every aspect of your personality, but it is necessary to see yourself as a complete and established entity. You need to be truthful to what you are – you need to respect yourself. Acting is not about *forgetting* who you are, but about *remembering* who you are and then *realizing* what you can become. Make-up and costume will aid you with your character work, but knowledge of yourself and your

abilities will serve you to become a very good actor indeed.

Attaining this self-knowledge cannot be achieved overnight or in any specific way. It is more about attaining a certain state of mind and following a path that leads you towards yourself rather than away.

KNOWING THE VOCAL YOU

Try the following experiment: sit yourself comfortably next to any kind of audio recording device, relax yourself fully and then record yourself speaking each of the following:

- two pages read from a classic serious novel
- two pages read from a modern comic novel

- an article read from a newspaper
- a long shopping list
- a day's viewing on one channel read from a television listings magazine
- an improvised account of your day so far – in the style of an audio diary.

As you speak these varied pieces allow yourself to 'feel' your voice working. Try to enhance your awareness of the texture of the sound you are making and to be in touch with the sensation of your speaking rather than just the sound of it. Be self-indulgent and wallow in the process; enjoy the sound you are making and have confidence in the authority of your voice; know that your voice is unique and beautiful and have pride in the sound.

Now listen to the recording you have made. At first, this will seem to undo completely what you have achieved. Everybody hates their voice on tape because they are used to hearing their voice internally as well as externally and, therefore, the recorded sound seems to lack resonance. But this is only an illusion caused by immediate comparison and if you persist in listening to your recorded voice, gradually you will begin to equate the sound with the feelings you experienced when making it. Through this process you will not only come to truly know your voice and how it sounds, but also to appreciate fully its qualities and potential.

Do not worry about analysing the good and the bad here – leave that to your specific voice work. Just concentrate on your overall voice at its present standard and just simply appreciate and accept it.

KNOWING THE PHYSICAL YOU

If you are able to enlist the help of a friend and a video camera have yourself videoed doing each of the following:

- walking at medium pace for approximately one hundred yards
- running at medium pace for the same distance
- dusting and vacuuming a room
- walking up and then down stairs
- throwing (and catching) a ball against a wall
- moving between all the seats in a room and sitting in each for a short while.

Treat this in exactly the same way as in the previous exercise: try to find a correlation between how your movement feels and what you see on the video. As before, try to look positively at yourself: get a feeling for how you move through space and for the uniqueness of your movement; get familiar with your shape (whatever this may be), and try to feel in tune with your body and how it inhabits the world.

If you find this exercise inhibiting with another person, set up the video on a tripod and try to film yourself. However, it is no bad thing to be aware of your movement whilst being watched by others.

KNOWING THE INNER YOU

This is probably the most important experiment of all. Make a list of at least four items in each of the following categories:

- good qualities that you possess
- areas in your personality that might need improvement
- personal ambitions
- things about yourself that you particularly like
- things about yourself that you would want to keep secret from others
- unique selling points about yourself
- bad habits and why you do them
- personal prejudices and why you have them

An actor must have belief in himself.

- ways in which you enhance the world you live in
- subjects that interest you passionately
- possessions you desire
- types of people that attract you.

It does not matter if there are replications amongst the lists. This is not about compiling numerous facts, but about looking at yourself in different ways and from different angles.

Now go back over your lists and edit them for truth. Cross out any that you do not truly believe, even if this reduces your answers below the minimum of four. When you are satisfied that these represent an honest view of yourself, use the information you have gathered to write a 300-word appraisal of 'you' the person and your present life.

Finally, learn the appraisal (not word for word, but the essence of it), and speak it as if making a presentation to an imaginary audience (or a real one if you wish). Doing this will lead you from the introspective of the task back into performance – for it is here that knowing who you are is vital in enabling you to know the characters that you act.

GROUP KNOWLEDGE

All three of these exercises are designed to be completed alone but can also be undertaken in a group situation. This would be achieved by

Many people see acting as an escape from themselves. Although there is certainly an element of this, it should never be your basic philosophy of acting. Face up to yourself; take a good long, hard look and be confident in what you see. Good and bad points are not of great relevance – the characters you play will have them too – but an understanding of who you are and what you have to offer is vital.

If you are serious about acting you will face a good deal of criticism over the years. Because your craft uses 'you' as its materials (unlike painting or sculpture), this criticism will feel personal and go deep. So, don't compound the problem by being too hard on yourself. Get up every morning, look in the mirror and rejoice in 'you' – a completely unique acting commodity. You should not become conceited or arrogant, but you should be fully in tune with yourself and proud of the contribution you can make to life and drama. Be constructive in developing and improving your personality, but try not to deal harshly with yourself – leave this to others.

From a belief in yourself and an understanding of your role in the world will spring truthful characterizations and great acting generally.

others feeding back on your discoveries about yourself and seeing where any discrepancies lay. However, if you do this, make a rule that you will all stay positive and not be overly critical of each other. This is all about having a realistic but appreciative understanding of yourself as a human being; it is not about reconstructing your personality. Proper acting stems from a knowledge of your worth as a person and an affirming attitude to your potential, not the reverse.

And remember, this work is designed only to give you a nudge in the right direction – feeling 'comfortable with yourself' is a life-long philosophy that every actor should instigate and then studiously follow.

BUILDING A CHARACTER

You must now start to concentrate on your approach to characterization itself. As with acting generally, this is both a technical exercise and an instinctive one. It has already been established that an actor only has him or herself to work with and that their characters must grow naturally from their own personalities. However, there are techniques and devices that can be employed to facilitate this process.

There are two main ways of approaching character work and both are worthy of your examination. It is not important which route you take – both lead you on a journey towards a complete practical understanding of the role you are playing – but it is important that you complete the journey.

INSIDE OUT

This method starts with the inner being of the person you are to act. At first, you should not be at all concerned with how this person walks, moves or talks; their appearance to the outside world is not of primary concern. You begin by finding out as much as possible about the personality of the person (and what motivates them to be as they are). It is important not to become pretentious in this: it is not about what brand of sausages they eat, although it may well be about whether they eat meat at all.

Some of your discoveries will arise from the play itself, others will stem from your imagination. However, be careful always to develop your characters honestly from what is written on the page: it is the job of the actor to interpret imaginatively but truthfully in harmony with the author, not to construct unilaterally.

From the knowledge and, more importantly, the understanding that you carefully assemble about the character, the process begins to move towards the outside. Slowly but surely you must allow the inner person to 'bleed' out into your body and voice. If you go carefully, this method will enable you

to not only be truthful to the character, but also allow you to play them organically from within yourself. You will find a way of being 'them' from within 'you'; you will 'rearrange' yourself without being forced to impose any particular characteristics that may lead you to perform rather than act.

This is certainly not a fast technique and will involve you in much work outside of rehearsals. Provided there is time, a good director will certainly incorporate such analysis as part of your company work together, but rehearsals are not just about you, and so much of your groundwork must be done alone and (if possible) in advance.

OUTSIDE IN

Obviously this is a reverse process. This time you commence with the outward appearance and sound of the person, and use this to work inward to an appreciation of their personalities. This is certainly a quicker, more

The 'biggest' of characters must be approached truthfully.

straightforward method, but be careful not to rush. It is usually better to begin with perhaps just one physical attribute (perhaps the walk) and build from there. Also, make sure that your physical vision of the character is supported by the text: this method is much more likely to lead you towards caricature and away from the truth if you are not careful.

We will now explore further each of these two techniques.

Exploring Inside Out

For this exercise you will need pen, paper and a comfortable chair. Please note from the outset that this is a slightly artificial exercise in that it is not based upon a character in any play. It is designed to get you thinking in the right way about your character work and will need a little adaptation when employed in your real work on text. In a sense, working on a play will be easier, as much of the work will be shared with the playwright.

Begin by selecting the memory of a person that you have met recently and who is the same sex as yourself. This should be a brief acquaintance – just long enough to form a general impression of the person. A good example might be someone who has served you in a shop. You will use the image of this person purely as a starting point. The character you build from here will, of course, be nothing like the person chosen (neither should they) – they are simply a means by which to start a process which will, from here on, rely totally on your personal imagination.

Now write down answers to all of the following questions. Remember, unlike when working on a play, you are building from scratch – all you have to work with is a fleeting overview of a person contained in your memory and from this you will give birth to a very specific fictitious character. The questions are asked (and should be answered) in three basic sets:

SET OF QUESTIONS – ONE

1. How old is the character?
2. What class do they belong to?
3. Where do they live?
4. Who do they live with?
5. What kind of house do they live in?
6. What is their job?
7. What is their ethnic background?
8. What sexual relationships do they have?
9. Who are their parents and what kind of relationship do they have with them?

Before moving on to the second set of questions it is worth making an important point about the second question in this set. Although today's citizens are supposed to be living in (or moving towards) a classless society, actors know that class is still a very important determining factor when building a characterization. Therefore, whatever your political view of the concept of class, you should not ignore its effect on the life of the character you are playing.

The next set of questions is a little more involved and should be answered more fully:

SET OF QUESTIONS – TWO

1. How positive or negative is their outlook on life?
2. How confident are they?
3. How kind or cruel are they?
4. How generous or mean are they (both in financial terms and spirit)?
5. How honest are they?
6. How tidy or messy are they?
7. What do they worry about?
8. How outgoing or introverted are they?
9. Are they aggressive or passive?
10. Are they caring or hard – loving or cold?
11. How organized or disorganized are they?
12. Are they a dreamer or down to earth?

There are many questions to be answered when characterizing.

7. Do they smoke and if so what?
8. What do they like and hate most?
9. What are their vices and virtues?
10. Do they have any disabilities?
11. What are their political views?
12. What are their religious views?
13. Are they artistic or more scientific in nature?
14. What qualifications do they have?

Each of these three sets of questions is designed to broaden your thinking about characterization. You will, by now, be building a person who, whilst totally fictitious, will have some real credibility within your imagination. Of course, these are not the only questions that could be asked but just examples, so now continue the process by asking and answering any further questions that you can think of in any or all of the sections.

Having done this, you will have developed quite an involved written portrait (albeit in note form), and all of this will have stemmed from a simple image of a person that you do not actually know. Finally, give them a name that you find artistically appropriate.

If you have the opportunity to work on this with friends, each member of the group should now verbally introduce their character to the others. You do not necessarily have to include all your answers but use them selectively to develop an overall picture. You should also ask supplementary questions of each other. This is not to catch each other out, but to stretch your imaginations as far as possible and to develop fully your theoretical character. If you are working alone dictate an introduction to your character on to tape or write it in the form of a short biography. The following may serve as an example:

The final set of questions is concerned with seemingly more superficial matters, but can still be answered quite thoughtfully and fully in light of the detail that has gone before:

SET OF QUESTIONS – THREE

1. What kind of car do they drive (and what colour is it)?
2. What kind of clothes do they wear?
3. What hobbies and entertainment do they enjoy?
4. What is their taste in décor?
5. What foods do they eat most?
6. Do they drink alcohol and if so what is their favourite tipple?

Mavis is a 68-year-old retired schoolteacher. She has always been single and has no children. She has a hard and aggressive manner, which hides a lack of self-worth and confidence. She is very old-fashioned in her outlook and complains about the 'youth of today' constantly. She likes music and reading, but her great love is photography and she is bitter that she was not able to follow this as a career due to her father's vehement opposition. She has a yellow car dating from the 1960s but rarely uses it these days. She used to enjoy travel, but is now in poor health and has become something of a recluse. She lives in a large Victorian terraced house in a provincial town, with a garden that she loves but is now far too large for her to keep properly.

The Character Emerges from the Page

This theory may now be put into practice, but it must be done so in a slow and careful way: it is vital at this stage to allow the physicality of the character to grow out of the work you have done so far.

Begin the next stage of this work by putting aside your pen and paper, freeing yourself of all encumbrances and exchanging your comfortable chair for a more upright one. As you sit in this chair, rearrange your position to be more in keeping with the way your character would sit. There may be quite a significant difference or little or no change at all. The important thing is not to force anything – just allow things to alter as required.

Be careful to have a purpose for sitting in the chair. In other words, imagine a situation for your character to be in as they sit there. Never act in a vacuum; always imagine a purpose and reason for what you do, even when working on exercises.

This can now be developed into movement. Stand up and walk around; remain in character and experiment with the how and why you move in a particular way. Do not be tempted to elaborate. Your character may very well move in a very similar (if not identical) way to you. As you feel more confident, start to do things: simple things, like switching on a light, moving a chair or looking out of a window. Remember always to have a reason in mind for what you do, and do not mime action. It is important that you remain as realistic as possible.

Quick Start Guide to Acting

13. Working Hard on Character

Always know as much as possible about the role that you are portraying. Read the play very carefully several times before the start of rehearsal and be aware of what the text means to you. Drama is about changing the lives of our audiences in some way – be it ever so little – and yours should be changed too. Make notes about your character and gather as much information from the playwright as is available within the script.

The playwright will not give you all the information you need; drama is a collaborative effort. Fill in the gaps in your character's life. Know for yourself exactly who the character is. Do this truthfully and don't go off at a tangent: you must be respectful to the text and keep your imaginative contribution within the bounds of what the author is trying to achieve. Work alongside the playwright and not in opposition; together you will achieve much. However, remember that you will not always be working with good scripts (sometimes they will be very poor); the worse the play, the more individual work on character and intention will be needed by you.

Actors can have fun bringing characters to life.

Now you are ready to experiment with voice. Imagine that your character is making or taking a telephone call and gently find the way that they speak. There may well be a change of accent from your own, but concentrate more on differences in rhythm and pace – their rate of thinking. Do not push; you only have the one voice, but experiment with differences of tone, pitch and emphasis. As before, let it come naturally and resist the temptation to caricature. Less really can be more.

You can continue this exercise by placing your character in some appropriate im-provisational situations. If you are working in a group, finish the exercise by 'hot-seating' your character. This is achieved by sitting alone in your chair and answering questions from the group in character. If working alone, imagine questions that might be put to you and answer them out loud, as if you are being interviewed on a chat show.

INVESTIGATING OUTSIDE IN

As well as working outside in now, you will also be working from the bottom up. In preparation, beg or borrow a pair of shoes of a style that you would not personally choose. This will be your starting point for another character.

Put on the shoes and simply walk about. Experiment with the feeling that the shoes give you and let that start to influence the way you walk. In order to kick-start the process of this exercise it is appropriate to exaggerate this just a little. Still working on the outside, now develop the movement and experiment with voice as you did for the latter parts of the 'Inside Out' exercise. The difference will be that now you are working instinctively. You have no idea why this character is beginning to take shape in this way – your only reference point at present is a pair of shoes. Really enjoy this process; have fun and play as a child might do when 'dressing-up'.

Return to the three sets of questions from the previous exercise and begin to answer them. Develop the character as before, but this time use the instinctive feel of the movement and sound you have created from the pair of shoes to guide you. Again, use improvisation and, in particular, hot-seating to aid you if you can.

QUICK START GUIDE TO ACTING

14. 'Growing' a Character

Do not force your body and voice to adopt the characteristics of the part you are playing, as this will lead to wooden and caricature-like acting. Let the role grow gradually and firmly. Let the knowledge you have gained about the character inform their appearance to the world, and try not to see your character as something that is acquired from outside of you. Practise the physical qualities in your own time. Rehearsal periods are seldom long enough and the more work you can do outside of them the better.

Always be true to the character in the way you do everything on stage. You do not necessarily have to be subtle in your characterization, but you do have to be honest.

Experimenting with characterization in public must not go too far.

TRUTHFUL CHARACTERS

From these two exercises you will have worked in reasonable depth upon two different characters. They may be very different to you or, indeed, very similar. This does not matter: the important thing is that they are truthful and part of you. You should not feel as if you are trying to make these characters as different as possible from you, but rather the opposite. Acting is concerned with reality and truth, and you should welcome and embrace the similarities to the real-life, living 'you'. However, as with all elements of acting, the truth can be pushed hard provided it is grounded in reality. You may be required to play parts that are very far away from your own personality, but you should never forget that you are the vehicle for these characters. It is you who brings them to the stage and, therefore, they must always be soundly rooted in you and who you are as a person.

OUT AND ABOUT

If you are brave enough, there is a very good way that you can test your work from this chapter. Choose one of the two characters you have developed and live them for a while in the real world: go shopping as them, for example. You will soon find out if you are resorting to caricature, as you will not be able to take your character out without feeling and appearing conspicuous. However, if the character is properly and organically rooted in you, as it should be, this will be perfectly possible to get away with without mishap or embarrassment. The 'danger' of this exercise will cause you to draw the character instinctively back towards yourself – and this is no bad thing. Provided you stay loyal to your character's motivations and agendas, you will find the exercise extremely affirming of your true acting ability. However, a word of warning: please do not attempt this with a character who is likely to offend someone overly much or break the law.

9 FACING THE AUDIENCE

BEING DYNAMIC

Apart from talent and technique, there is one other supreme factor that determines the accomplished and successful actor, and that is their 'stage presence'. It is difficult sometimes to analyse just exactly what this quality is, but it is very much easier to recognize it. You will have noticed how some actors seem to draw your attention to them from the moment they walk out upon the stage; how they seem to exude a personality fuelled with energy and brightness; how they appear to be so at home on stage that they might almost have been born there. It may be less immediately apparent, but true nonetheless, that these actors are always somehow 'likable'; they never fail to endear themselves to their audience, even if the character they are portraying is in theory unpleasant and unsympathetic. In short, actors who have this 'presence', whatever it may actually be, are able to win you over and make you want to know what they are about, sometimes even before they have actually said or done anything.

Although this is a quality that comes quite naturally to some and less so to others, it can to a certain extent be developed, or at least improved upon. To a very large extent it is a quality that is directly related to the actor's own personal 'energy' and how they use it. In order for you to develop your own stage presence you will need to examine this energy in yourself, and to do this properly you will also need a very clear understanding of what is meant by an actor's energy in the first place.

Energy as a scientific concept can have many practical understandings within our daily lives. Energy in acting is about mental energy and concentration. An actor's use of energy concerns the filling of text with thought and purpose, and the projection of that energy in varying degrees of size and power.

BUBBLES OF ENERGY AND THOUGHT

'Bubbles of energy and thought' is a concept, a metaphorical way of thinking, which will aid you enormously with the production and control of energy in your work. There are three bubbles to think about and, although they exist only in your mind, they will have a greater practical effect upon the quality of your acting than any other device that you employ. The benefits of these 'bubbles' may not be immediately apparent and it may take you a while to appreciate exactly what they are and how you can use them. However, persevere – for they will help you to be more dynamic and engaging on stage that you ever thought

possible. The First Bubble is a bubble that simply exists around you; a bubble that you exist inside alone. The Second Bubble is the First Bubble extended to enclose you and other characters in the scene you may be interacting with. The Third Bubble, and perhaps the most important of all, is a bubble that surrounds you and everything and everyone in the theatre. It is important to examine each of these separately and then see how they work together as a whole.

THE FIRST BUBBLE

This bubble allows you to focus upon your own personal energy and how it can radiate from you and surround you; it is about your ability to concentrate your thoughts and intentions and project them outwards. In developing the strength of mental energy required you will focus all of your thousands of communication devices into a forceful whole. Your audiences will be compelled to look at you and become subconsciously captivated by your actions on stage; they will want to see what you are to say and do; they will instinctively care about your character's relevance to the plot and progress within the play. In a sense, it is nothing more than the power of thought, but the benefits can be enormous.

In life, people who possess dynamic and appealing personalities are usually those who are fuelled by great amounts of energy. This energy may not necessarily manifest itself in extrovert exuberance, but the person concerned will be enthusiastic, highly charged and positive in their approach to life. This is

*OPPOSITE: **The power of energy and concentration.***

how you must be on stage – not as the character, who may well be of a very different personality, but as the actor behind the character. The 'bubble' technique, and in particular the First Bubble, will help you to tap into your own personal energy source and achieve this.

To experience and experiment with the First Bubble, sit comfortably in a chair and consciously relax your body and mind. Begin by imagining that your whole body is a very powerful light bulb that continues to grow brighter and brighter the longer it is switched on. Concentrate your mind on this imaginary light and make it as real for yourself as you possibly can. Imagine that your light is shining so brightly that any person who might see it would be drawn towards it. With the light, feel also the tremendous warmth that you are creating and bask in its power as it radiates from you.

Now use the power of your imagination to create a bubble around you and the chair you are sitting in; a bubble which completely contains you and the immediate space around you. This bubble is not perfectly round but is flexible, and can stretch around you. Fill this bubble with the light from you, the imaginary source of it; do not let the light travel outside of the bubble, but continue to glow brighter so that the space within the bubble glows more and more with each passing second. If you find that your mind is wandering from this task, refocus it and constantly re-engage your concentration upon making the bubble around you special and dynamic.

Try to concentrate upon the whole space within the bubble. Let your thoughts continuously focus upon the walls of the bubble in front of you, at your sides, above your head and beneath your feet. Even the places you cannot actually see (behind you) must be strong in your thoughts. However, do not let your mind wander to the world outside of the bubble as before. Finish by sitting down again and re-energizing the bubble to its former brightness.

Using the First Bubble

As well as strengthening your concentration and increasing your mental energy, this exercise is extremely practical when speaking text. The state of focus that the First Bubble leads you into is exactly applicable to the speaking of soliloquies or when your character is speaking to another but is drawing the thoughts back and internalizing the emotion (in other words, speaking to themself even though there is another person present listening).

As an example of this, consider very carefully the following speech and, if possible, commit it to memory:

> I never saw him again. I suppose, if I am honest, I knew then that we were saying goodbye for the last time. He was so calm, you see; as if he understood exactly what he had to do and had already made up his mind to do it. I just didn't realize; I was so wrapped up in my own problems I couldn't see the obvious; I was totally oblivious to what was staring me right in the face. He looked strange, yes, but I had seen him look like that before. You know how he used to look sometimes when he was pleased with himself about something; sort of contented – well, he looked like that. I always see him like that now when I think of him. I'll never forget the way he looked that night.

An actor in 'First Bubble'.

bubble; nothing in the universe should exist for you except the bubble and you inside of it. Although you may close your eyes in order to help marshal your thoughts, do not do so all of the time; look around you, but without allowing your eyes to focus beyond the bubble.

The next stage is to stand up and walk around. The shape of the bubble in your mind is flexible and will move with you, except that now it will be a more angular shape as it continues to surround your body. Obviously, it will not be possible to remain totally focused within the bubble, otherwise you will bump into things, but try to let your concentration extend only as far as is necessary for practicality and safety, and keep the bulk of your thought and energy contained within the

Before you go any further, decide what this speech actually means. There are several possible interpretations that might be truthful to the text, but it doesn't matter how you interpret it as long as it means something specific in your mind. Remember, you cannot act in a vacuum: you must always know what you are saying and why you are saying it. If it suits your interpretation of the speech, you can change the person you are talking about to female, but try, as always, to say all of the other words correctly without paraphrasing. Learning it will make it much easier to act than if reading.

Now practise the speech while existing inside of your imaginary First Bubble. There should definitely be a listener present, and if this can be a friend rather than an imaginary person so much the better. However, your thoughts must never reach them; they will be extremely strong thoughts and they will be very apparent to any audience, but they will be internalized, with your mental and visual focus stopping short at the walls of the bubble. The thrust of your acting will be that the emotion has allowed you to forget the person that you are talking to and, although the narrative is strong, the words are almost entirely for your own benefit.

Remember to equate your concentration to light, so that, although the speech will seem naturally withdrawn, it will also project outwards towards the audience, albeit an imaginary one. Don't rush; savour the main objective of the speech, which is the remembrance and absolution of past emotion.

THE SECOND BUBBLE

In order to now move on you will again need the help of a friend if possible. If this is not possible get hold of the largest teddy bear, doll or manikin that you can and use it as a reasonably tangible (if less responsive) partner.

Place this real or substitute partner in another chair, sitting approximately four feet away from you and reasonably in line with the way you are facing. Begin by strongly establishing your First Bubble once again and then, when it is good and strong, mentally extend the bubble forwards to envelop your partner in the other chair. This Second Bubble is not separate from the first but purely an extension of it. However, you now have a bigger space to fill with your energy; the metaphorical light has been diluted so it must burn all the brighter in order not to lose its overall strength. Concentrate now on the area of this bigger bubble and fill every part of it with your thoughts just as you did before.

A potential audience would now not only be fascinated by you but by the object of your attention; your character becomes irresistible to them, as do the objectives of that character's life within the play.

Now stand up and walk around the chair in which your partner is sitting, letting the bubble move with you and ensuring that the two of you remain in it at all times. Your own personal dynamism is now mobile and readily includes anything that you choose to include in the focus of your attention. Extend your practice of this to more partners (just use chairs if you run out of friends or stuffed toys) and work on keeping your bubble 'strong', however many other imaginary characters may be contained within it.

To recap: your First Bubble always contains just you; your Second Bubble contains you and those on the stage with you who are included in your mental focus.

Using the Second Bubble

Look at the speech written out again: you will see that now certain parts of it are in brackets. As you work through it again, allow your First Bubble to extend into the Second as you reach the bracketed parts, and return to the First as the brackets close. This will have the effect of shifting your focus from introverted thought to moments of 'reaching out' your communication to the single partner; in acting terms you will cross between talking to yourself and talking to your partner.

However, in addition, the focus and dynamism of your energy and concentration will change too and this will direct and lead the audience through the speech in a most focused way. You should find that practising this, coupled with your usual attention to the thoughts and motivations behind the text, will shape and structure the speech almost automatically and make it extremely 'watchable':

I never saw him again. I suppose, if I am honest, I knew then that we were saying goodbye for the last time. (*He was so calm, you see; as if he understood exactly what he had to do and had already made up his mind to do it.*) I just didn't realize; (*I was so wrapped up in my own problems*) I couldn't see the obvious; I was totally oblivious to what was staring me right in the face. He looked strange, yes, but I had seen him look like that before. (*You know how he used to look sometimes when he was pleased with himself about something; sort of contented – well, he looked like that.*) I always see him like that now when I think of him. I'll never forget the way he looked that night.

You may find that the swapping in and out of the two bubbles seems a little forced at first, but persevere and you will find the process becoming smoother and smoother. You will quickly become accomplished at it and you will find the technique a perfect blend of truthful emotion and technical expertise.

The next step is to change the places where you extend into the Second Bubble. Find the points in the text that seem right for you and experiment with how by changing the bubble you can alter the dynamics of the speech. Finally, try the speech while walking around instead of sitting still, or even a mixture of both; make sure that you can change bubbles independently of your changes of movement. Do not forget that, in a scene, your partner would have his or her own Second Bubble that would add to the power of yours.

THE THIRD BUBBLE

This is the most important bubble of the three. Unlike the other two, which never exist at the same time together, the Third Bubble is always

One actor in 'First Bubble', one in 'Second'.

present and, in fact, bubbles One and Two exist within it constantly. You will see how this works practically later, but for the time being you must think of the Third Bubble in isolation.

Return to your chair and concentrate upon the bright light emanating from you, just as you have done each time. As usual, begin slowly and gradually increase the brightness of the light as your concentration settles. However, this time allow your bubble to expand much further until it fills the whole room. The bigger the room the better, for the exercise here is to discipline your mind to remain focused on as big an area as possible. Keep thinking about everything within this bubble, even those things that may be behind you. There will be quite a lot of the room that you will not be able to see, but you will know what it looks like nonetheless and you should try to be constantly aware and thoughtful of everything in this much enlarged bubble.

When you are acting, this bubble is always there and encompasses the whole of the theatre, including the stage you are on and, of course, the audience. The walls of the bubble must extend to the very reaches of the auditorium, so that even those in the back row of the 'gods' are contained within it. Your other two circles will work away within it, but it is ever active and means that a part of your mind will always be concerned with the entire space that your performance exists in. This Third Bubble has three very important applications:

1. It enhances your stage presence and beams yours personality to the very back of the theatre.
2. It ensures that however much your concentration may be engaged in acting the part you are playing, a portion of your mind will always be aware of the audience and the fact that everything you are doing

QUICK START GUIDE TO ACTING

15. Balancing Energy

It is not only important for actors to possess mental, physical and emotional energy themselves, but they must also be able to identify the various energies within a scene and know how to work with them. Acting energy, as a whole, tends to remain constant, with changes occurring only in the manner that energy is channelled at any given moment: in other words, the balance of the energy changes.

As an example of this, during a long speech in which a character is in a constant state of extreme anger, much of the dialogue may be extremely loud. However, there may be times when the actor wishes to reduce the volume, but, in doing so (and in order to maintain the required level of anger), his or her voice may become far more menacing and intense. The volume will have decreased, but that energy will have manifested itself in another way – thus remaining constant. Control of energy in this way helps an actor to be dynamic and irresistibly appealing in their telling of the story.

is for them. It also helps you to be sensitive to the way they are receiving your work.

3. It automatically tailors the projection of your performance (including, but not exclusively, your voice) to the size of the auditorium. Thus you can avoid over- or under-projection of your performance.

The Third Bubble is very much about the strength of your concentration. Practise it in ever bigger rooms and even look out of a window and try to include the entire view

'Third Bubble' may be practised outside.

(however far) within the bubble. If you feel your mind wandering, just refocus it as before and keep trying to include the whole area in your thoughts.

PRACTISING ALL THREE BUBBLES

Revisit the work you did on Bubbles One and Two, only this time imagine them to be inside the larger and ever constant third. Rehearse the speech again in this way, making sure that some of your concentration remains within the far reaches of the Third Bubble. The first two bubbles change and flow within the ever

constant third, and all the bubbles are continuously filled with your own vital energy.

Continue to practise this technique with as many different texts and in as many different spaces as you can. The more your mind becomes used to the amount and flexibility of concentration that is needed, the better you will be able to put these skills to use when you step upon a stage for real.

As you should have already discovered, this technique is as much concerned with your awareness of an audience as it is with the structuring of your performance energy. This awareness will of course be very much in the back of your mind at an almost subconscious level, but its existence will allow you to monitor the 'feel' of the audience. You will be able to sense when they are 'with you' and when you may be 'losing them'; you will know when to increase your energy or pace to pull back their attention; you will begin to develop an instinctive ability to focus their attention on what you are trying achieve in the play. However, the most important factor here is that you will be able to do all this while still apportioning the majority of your concentration on delivering an honest and truthful interpretation of your role.

THE IMPORTANCE OF PERSEVERANCE

There can be no doubt that the work of this chapter can appear strange and even pretentious. It is probably the least straightforward of the acting techniques and probably the least easily accessible. Very often as you practise these bubbles you will feel silly and uncomfortable, and your mind will start to question the relevance of what you are doing. Do not allow this to put you off: keep working on the techniques and keep them in mind whenever you start to work on a new play. It may well be a while before you start to appreciate the benefits on offer here, but one day things will click into place and you will suddenly realize what a practical and down-to-earth tool these seemingly 'ethereal' bubbles can be. Persevere and you really will find yourself not only being far more dynamic on stage, but you will also acquire an admirable ability to technically control everything you do, freeing you completely to be real and truthful in your acting.

10   TAMING SHAKESPEARE

DISCOVERING THE ADVANTAGE OF GENIUS

It is unlikely that William Shakespeare could have foreseen the amount of trepidation he would cause amongst some actors in the twenty-first century. He would have been appalled to discover that his work was considered to be difficult to understand, complicated and inaccessible. After all, despite being the artistically poetic genius that he was, he was writing very much for a popular audience. For pure economic expediency, his plays needed to talk directly to an audience in terms they could readily identify with: it had to be obviously relevant to their lives; exciting and stimulating while at the same time remaining down to earth; as well as clearly plotted and easily understandable to people of every class and education. Shakespeare's work did all of this, but, more importantly for the modern actor, it still does.

It is largely because Shakespeare achieved these objectives that he became a celebrated and successful playwright. However, it is also the reason that his work has transcended the years to make him arguably the greatest writer who ever lived. In basic terms, Shakespeare's plays are just as relevant, pertinent and accessible as they ever were. Why then is the reverse often believed? Why is Shakespeare considered to be so 'difficult'? This may be partly because many people are introduced to the plays in an academic context at school: they begin by reading the plays in a dull and uninspiring way. Even when they get the chance to see the plays performed, the interpretation may be equally lacking in imaginative expertise. However, there is probably another, more fundamental reason for Shakespeare's 'bad press'. It can be very easy to get bogged down in the seeming complexity of Shakespearian language and sentence construction; the plays seem to present themselves in a way that is alien to our modern dramatic culture. However, this is just a 'smoke screen' caused by adopting a particular view of the text. A simple adjustment of perspective will reveal the content of the plays to be breathtakingly clear, and, more importantly, strikingly ill-uminating of the human condition in a modern world.

It is the job of actors and directors to focus the material in a way which disarms the various trivial difficulties that can add up to create an insuperable effect of complexity; they must angle the work so that its clarity and transparent meaning can be viewed. However, before this can be achieved they must find this clarity of view themselves, by looking beneath the surface that can initially seem so distracting in order to recognize the true purpose of the text. Most of what seems

OPPOSITE: *Shakespeare's genius makes acting easier, not harder.*

complicated and indiscernible is actually just the result of misunderstanding the slightly different way in which Shakespeare formulated the thoughts and intentions of his characters. Once this is understood, the actor can interpret and communicate the text in an extremely straightforward way. True, there may also be words whose meaning is not readily discernible, but most editions of Shakespeare have accompanying notes which solve this problem. The main task for the actor therefore is to do exactly as in every other type of play – apply their technique to identify the character and their character's thought processes and intentions. In other words, the approach is no different to any other work.

JUST ANOTHER JOB

While it may be true that interpreting Shakespeare is merely the application of a process that an actor applies to all drama, it is also easy to perceive it as a more difficult task. However, once inside the Shakespearian mindset, the actor discovers that everything needed to bring the characters and situations to life is laid out in majestic simplicity and clarity. As the fear drops away comes the realization that Shakespeare's skill as a wordsmith makes the job of acting his work far easier than that of a lesser playwright. Indeed, it is bad writers who are hard to act: they provide two-dimensional characters, gaps in plots and inconsistencies of emotional development, all of which have to be rectified by the actor. In contrast, the good writers do so much more of the work and present far superior materials for the actor to use in the construction of a living reality; it follows therefore that the finest of them all should be the easiest to approach. If the actor believes this and views the Shakespearian penmanship as a colossal advantage, then they will be well on the way to forging a partnership with the writer that will lead to some truly wonderful performances.

As you approach Shakespeare, concentrate not upon any fear you may have for the genre, but simply upon the techniques you have learnt. As you apply them you will grow in confidence and the process of interpreting such great work will improve your ability to act using any text. There will be three main aims for you as you study Shakespeare: firstly, to identify and eradicate all areas of potential misunderstanding and alienation; secondly, to formulate your basic 'map of thoughts', motivations and intentions; and thirdly, to realize the potential for bringing naturalism, realism and truth to the scenes when they are taken to the stage with other characters and given life.

In order to discover how this works in practice it will be necessary for you to look at a short example from a Shakespearian play. Although this is a speech for a female actor, it is a character in the guise of a man and can therefore be played by a man for the exercise; it has, in fact, been portrayed by a male actor in past productions. Studying the scene will give a rounded illumination to both sexes of the task of acting Shakespeare.

ROSALIND FROM *AS YOU LIKE IT*

In this speech (Act III, Scene V) Rosalind, disguised as a man, has been secretly listening to a shepherdess (Phebe) berating her suitor, a shepherd (Silvius). As the speech begins she steps forward from her hiding place and takes great pleasure in informing Phebe of her opinion on the matter.

Read the speech in its entirety at first and do not worry about anything you do not understand. Just aim to get a general feeling for the shape of Rosalind's thought processes:

And why, I pray you? Who might be your mother,

That you insult, exult, and all at once,

Over the wretched? What, though you have no beauty –

As, by my faith, I see no more in you

Than without candle may go dark to bed –

Must you be therefore proud and pitiless?

Why, what means this? Why do you look on me?

I see no more in you than in the ordinary

Of nature's sale-work. 'Od's my little life,

I think she means to tangle my eyes too!

No, 'faith, proud mistress, hope not after it:

'Tis not your inky brows, your black silk hair,

Your bugle eyeballs, nor your cheek of cream

That can entame my spirits to your worship.

There is so much for the modern actor to identify with here, not least the immense feeling of freedom that Rosalind experiences in being able to take control of the situation because she is a man – or appears to be. She takes great delight in ignoring all of the ladylike manners and virtues that would normally apply to her, by being rude, direct and, most importantly, in command. It is remarkable to find a strong feminist theme

QUICK START GUIDE TO ACTING

16. Shakespearian Rules

When approaching a Shakespearian text remember the following points:

1. Do not be frightened of Shakespeare – he is actually the most actor-friendly playwright of them all.
2. Do not make the mistake of thinking that Shakespearian plays are written in a kind of English that is difficult to understand – don't panic, use a good set of notes and accept and get used to the way that Shakespeare constructed his language. Once you are inside his head all will appear much clearer.
3. Banish any thought from your mind that Shakespeare is remote and irrelevant. His plays tackle subjects that are applicable to the experiences of all modern people. If you look at his plays without prejudice you will find a myriad of recognizable examples of human existence, often expanded into grand and dramatic themes.
4. Do not think that Shakespearian verse will make the parts more difficult to act: if you let it, the verse will carry you, support you, help you to find the right emphasis within the text, and generally aid you in finding truth in everything you say and do.
5. Watch good Shakespearian actors and see how they make every line crystal clear in both meaning and intention.

coming from a playwright long dead and who had no female actors at all in his company. The relevance of this theme wings its way through countless generations and gives the actor a strong and recognizable focus to playing the speech from the outset. Male actors, playing this speech as an exercise, can gain a useful insight into the powerfulness of many of Shakespeare's men (and also his women).

Shakespeare is also saying something about class here. You will notice that, despite being a basically decent individual at heart, Rosalind feels no inhibition about playing with the emotions of people she would instinctively consider inferior to her. Once again, Shakespeare talks directly to the actor through the years and supplies even more raw material to inform modern acting.

The speech is in a very common Shakespearian text form, that of Iambic Pentameter. This simply means that as a general (though not exclusive) rule, the lines are divided into five metrical feet, with each foot consisting of an unstressed and then stressed syllable or beat. The verse is also mainly (though again not exclusively) blank; in other words, there is no obvious rhyming structure.

The fact that so much of Shakespeare is in verse frightens many actors immensely. This is a pity, as it actually provides a perfect structure with which to shape the acting of the text. You must let the verse form be your friend. Trust it and let it lead your thoughts and intentions – the musicality and rhythm, far from distracting you, will focus you towards the core meaning and emphasis of each phrase.

So, as you work through the text now in more detail, concentrate on the wealth of feeling and motivation that Rosalind encounters, and allow this, coupled with the flow of the verse, to lead you to act with great clarity and detail.

MAKING THE TEXT WORK FOR YOU

'And why, I pray you? Who might be your mother'. This could not be a better first line because it gives you a solid first thought that is eminently contemporary in its simplicity: *Who the hell do you think you are?* Remember that this evolves from a moment of decision for Rosalind: she has chosen to begin an act of bravado completely alien to her usual experience, and so the line will be charged with energetic anticipation as she steps from her hiding place to confront the shepherdess.

'*That you insult, exult, and all at once, over the wretched?*' The first part of this line is a simple thought literally meaning that the shepherdess criticizes and then praises the shepherd at the same time ('all at once'). However, a more straightforward thought for you to play is: *Why do you keep messing him about?* The last three words are equally as clear, but are a good example of how expectation of the shaping of language, in modern terms, may confuse you: wretched should describe something ('wretched man' in this case), but here it is used to act as a descriptive name for the shepherd on its own. However, you can use the basic feeling of the word to inform the way you play it: therefore, as you say 'the wretched?' you can actually play the thought *poor devil* – or a less polite version if you prefer.

'*What, though you have no beauty –*'. The first word here is another example of how you might be misled: the word 'what' is not used directly to make the phrase a question, but as a simple exclamation to emphasize what follows. Such a small detail can lead off in completely the wrong direction, making what follows nonsensical, but keep your wits about you and you will avoid such pitfalls. The rest of the phrase is obvious in its meaning and will give you a wonderful opportunity to play the relish with which Rosalind experiments with her new-found rudeness and self-possession.

'*As, by my faith, I see no more in you than without candle may go dark to bed –*'. Another more obvious exclamation leads to a beautiful

'And why, I pray you? Who might be your mother.'

compounding of the previous rudeness. Shakespeare uses words so well that it is utterly forgivable that here (as so often) he uses several 'flowery' examples to communicate a very simple sentiment: the accepted meaning is that Phebe's beauty will not shine bright enough to make a candle unnecessary for her journey to bed. It is interesting to note that a modern playwright might have said go to bed in the dark, while Shakespeare reverses the construction of the phrase. You must get used to these reversals, as they happen often; do not let the unfamiliarity of construction and use of vocabulary blind you to the obvious and often pedestrian meanings in the text.

Feel free to embellish Shakespeare's meanings with your own. For instance, it is not unreasonable to play this line differently – as an insinuation that if Phebe slept with a man the lights would need to be extinguished to hide her ugliness. This is probably not what Shakespeare meant, but he did intend the scene to explore Rosalind's experimentation with manly vulgarity in every sense and, as the sentiment fits the lines, this alternative meaning can really work as a strong thought for you to play.

It is important for you to know that Rosalind is very aware that her cousin Celia is watching these proceedings and that she is already mightily amused by Rosalind's predicament of male impersonation. Therefore, there can start to emerge a strong intention of 'entertaining' Celia still further at this point, and this will give an added impetus and reality to your thoughts.

However you play this line, draw Phebe into a very tight Second Bubble with you (*see* Chapter 9), developing an almost conspiratorial element to your insults. If you vary this with occasional looks in the direction of Celia, you will find yourself warming to the task of creating the sense of mischief, daring and growing abandonment that the speech requires.

'*Must you be therefore proud and pitiless?*' This is a consummate phrase, both in its simple rhythmic construction and clever choice of opposing words. However, do not lose sight of the fact that its meaning is basic and so is the intention behind it. Your thought here is in essence exactly as the words obviously state, but it can be heavily tinged with distaste in the form of *you stupid girl* or, again, something more vulgar. Do not be awestruck by the excellence of these, or any other, Shakespearian words. It is your job at this stage to make the words unimportant but to give great importance to the thoughts behind them. Paradoxically, it is by doing this that you ultimately give the words the majesty on stage that they deserve.

'*Why, what means this? Why do you look on me?*' This is a perfect example of acting as a communal activity. Hopefully, if you were actually rehearsing or performing this scene, the actor playing Phebe would be reacting strongly to you and giving you a visual impetus for this line. In the play, Rosalind's manly show of arrogance has enchanted Phebe and she becomes hypnotically attracted to her (or 'him' as she sees it). Therefore, the line must be played with suspicion and the beginning of realization, but also it will be effective if you feel distracted and put-off a little from your previous confidence.

'*I see no more in you than in the ordinary of nature's sale work...*' This is obviously another insult, meaning Phebe to be akin to 'ready-made goods' and therefore inferior in quality.

But the important thing to play here is Rosalind's attempt to get her insults back on track while still being concerned about Phebe's amorous reaction. You are saying one thing while the focus of your thoughts is elsewhere.

'*Od's my little life, I think she means to tangle my eyes too!*' This starts with another exclamation meaning roughly, 'God save me!' It can be played strongly to pre-empt the full realization that is to come, or it can be quickly thrown away. As a general rule many actors attempt to place too much emphasis upon these exclamations, oaths and profanities that litter Shakespeare's plays, forgetting how they so often pepper modern speech. Do not get bogged down by them, but see them as connectors between thoughts and springboards into new thoughts.

The rest of the line marks Rosalind's complete realization that Phebe is 'making eyes' at her. It can be said as an aside either to the audience or to Celia, or may be played firmly without any attempt to conceal the thought from Phebe. Whichever you choose, it is vital that you realize that Rosalind is more amused than concerned: she knows that, as the man, she is in control and Phebe's confusion will not pose a threat. Allow this amusement to push up your energy and take the speech hereafter to a higher level of strutting arrogance.

'*No 'faith, proud mistress, hope not after it:*' Rosalind is of course trying to dissuade Phebe from her admiration, but there is also a light-hearted bawdy resonance to this: let your thoughts contain an element of ribald mirth, insinuating that she will be getting more than she bargained for. There is so much earthy wit in Shakespeare both stated and implied: you must identify it and play it strongly, for it is one of the things that will connect you to the present day.

'*'Tis not your inky brows, your black silk hair, your bugle eyeballs, nor your cheek of cream that can entame my spirits to your worship.*' This is a

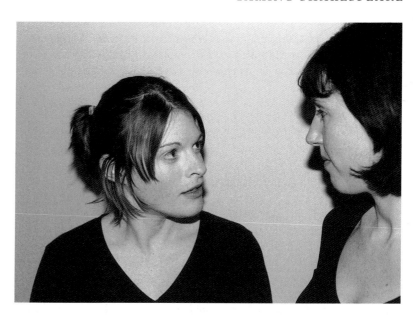

'I think she means to tangle my eyes too!'

list of attributes that a Shakespearian woman might think attractive to men. However, there is more to it than this, for Rosalind is feeling particularly antagonistic towards men at this stage of the play; you should therefore play this as a sarcastic liturgy to the weakness of women in wanting to ensnare men in such superficial ways. Remember also that there is a continuation of the amusement that started in the line before and that Rosalind is still strongly playing to the appreciative audience of Celia.

CONTINUING FROM HERE

There is another half to this speech, as Rosalind turns her attention to the shepherd, Silvius. Find a copy of the play and construct your own map of thought patterns for the remainder, always applying the principle of identifying what is behind each phrase and word. However, the trick of this is to look for the ordinary and pedestrian, for that is

basically what is there and is the key that will unlock your acting of Shakespeare.

Try to learn the complete speech and then act it through with a colleague playing Phebe and, if possible, another giving reaction as Celia. The golden rule is the same as with any playwright; play the speech in real time, giving as much attention to your fellows as you do to your own thoughts. The art of the actor is to make the text live, and no text will take life off the page more readily than Shakespeare's.

Now move on to experiment with as many scenes from Shakespeare as you can. A final word of warning though: do not read Shakespeare from a *Complete Works*. This may be a cheap way of obtaining all the plays (and it is useful to have one for reference), but the small print and crammed text will make you feel that you are undertaking a mammoth task. Find a good edition of the play you are working on, with a small amount of text on each page and plenty of notes.

11   ACTING COMEDY

IS COMEDY A SEPARATE TECHNIQUE?

It is a common belief that comedy requires exactly the same skills as all acting. It is certainly true that comedy requires all of the techniques you have learnt in the chapters of this book and applies them in much the same way. There is also no doubt that comedy requires just as much attention to reality, naturalness and, above all, truth. However, there is a difference, which manifests itself not so much as an alternative to acting technique, but as an important and exacting addition to it.

When playing comedy it is necessary to take all of the usual elements and techniques of acting and simply heighten them. In effect, comedy is a slightly heightened form of reality, which is reflected in an actor's approach to it. There is an additional requirement: to take a technical view of a scene in terms of where, and to what extent, laughs may be obtained. This is an obvious application of the Two-Brain Theory – the Technical Brain identifies a

comic moment and the Truth Brain finds a truthful way of obtaining it.

In order to explore the skills you will need to be successful as an actor in comedy, you will need to examine some basic comic concepts.

The basis of much comedy is found in pantomime. It is obviously a subject in itself, but for your purposes here it will only be necessary to concentrate upon the set gags and routines that form the backbone of pantomime comedy. These are extremely formulaic, but contain the very basics of comedy technique. Although each is different in content, the fundamentals are the same and a short study of one of the commonest will make an excellent example of this form of comedy and, indeed, comedy in general. As you examine it, look out for many principles that are found in all forms of comic performance. Although the genre of pantomime is two-dimensional and full of caricature, the successful execution of its comedy still requires adherence to the rules of truth and reality.

THE GHOST GAG

This requires a minimum of four people. As you initially think it through as a group, populate your minds with sufficient panto-mimic characters to make it work. The format of this gag can transpose into many situations

OPPOSITE: Comedy comprises words and action.

but remains essentially the same. This example is one of many possible manifestations:

Three people are waiting at a bus stop late at night. They are all feeling cold and occupying themselves by respectively reading a newspaper, listening to a Walkman and making a mobile telephone call. A ghost appears, creeps up to them and taps the shoulder of the person at the end of the queue. This person looks at the ghost, screams in terror and runs off. The ghost then taps the shoulder of the next person in the queue. This person also looks at the ghost, screams in terror and runs off. The ghost then taps the shoulder of the third and final person in the queue. This person looks at the ghost as the others have done, but this time it is the ghost that screams in terror and runs away.

Although the basic plot of this routine is extremely simple, there are some important points to make about it, which illuminate some fundamental principles of comedy and comic acting.

It is vital that the three characters are preoccupied with something so that they are unaware of what is happening to the others until it happens to them. The audience must believe that there is a reason for the monster to be able to surprise its victims. Although these reasons may be far-fetched and stretch credibility, they are rooted in truth and this will suffice to create a form of reality. Without this reality, the scene, and most comedy in general, will not work. An audience must be provided with an identifiable framework in order to relate to what they see and find it funny. Even the most bizarre comedy must have a link, however tenuous, to truth in this way if it is to be successful. It is extremely interesting for the actor to realize once again the unavoidable importance of truth in everything he or she does.

It is also important for there to be a good reason for the ghost to be afraid of the third person in the queue. In pantomime, this person would normally be the Dame (a comedy character played by a man dressed as a woman) and the comic implication would be that her extreme ugliness would frighten even a ghost. Without this rationale the joke is simply not funny and the scene is lost.

THE 'RULE OF THREE'

It is not accidental that there are three victims of the ghost. Three seems to be a magic number in comedy and very often scenes and gags work best in threes. Although nobody has quite worked out exactly why this is, there is certainly more than a clue in this scene: the first victim establishes the situation; the second victim confirms and creates a recognizable convention; while the third victim breaks the convention and 'pays off' the laugh. In other words, 'three' provides the audience with enough information to appreciate the joke without spoiling it with repetition. Although four victims could be used in this scene if absolutely necessary, five would kill the laugh stone dead. You will see in this that comedy must contain enough information and truth, but not too much.

The simplicity of the plot in this scene must be matched by clarity of action. Everything must be very clear and precise – the taps upon shoulders, the looks and the screams must all be executed cleanly, without any ambiguity or 'fussiness'. It is this that will lead an audience safely through the joke towards the laugh. Much of the actor's job in comedy is concerned with manoeuvring an audience in this way, and it requires the actor to maintain a clear focus upon the important elements of the scene. If there is too much extraneous information the audience's attention may wander from the essential element of the laugh just at the wrong moment. Rhythm is also important here and the actors must build the scene towards its comic climax, making sure that the pace is exactly right in order to build the audience's anticipation of laughter. Comedy is about knowing when to 'allow' the audience to laugh and when to deny them the opportunity in order to increase expectation.

THE 'TAKE' AND THE 'DOUBLE TAKE'

The Ghost Gag can be elaborated upon by adding a 'take', which is a device that is not only native to this kind of pantomimic comedy, but also fundamental to the principles of comedy generally. This can be employed when any of the participants see the ghost. It is achieved by the actor looking at the ghost but not at first registering its significance; they turn away, only to realize suddenly what they have seen and then look back quickly with the appropriate reaction of shock and fear – thus completing 'the take'.

Once again, truth is the key to success here. The audience must believe that the pre-occupation of whatever the character has been doing while in the queue has genuinely slowed their awareness of what they are seeing. The moment of realization and subsequent reaction must be equally clear and founded in reality. As with all comedy, an audience will laugh at this mainly because they recognize something of which they have personal experience: everybody is prone to sometimes reacting slowly to a stimulus while their minds have been preoccupied elsewhere.

If you have been experimenting with performing the Ghost Gag, do it again, this time inserting the 'take' and trying to make it work effectively. The secret to your success will depend upon your ability to apply the usual acting technique of looking, thinking and reacting, but doing so in a perfectly natural and not stilted way – see the ghost,

register its presence but not its significance, let your mind swing immediately back to what is occupying it (listening to music, reading or even looking at the passing traffic), and then suddenly let your mind flood with realization and reaction. The physical requirement of turning your head towards the ghost, away again and then sharply back should happen and flow quite naturally from the process of your thoughts.

A 'double take' is the same device, but with an extra 'take' added. After the first look at the ghost, you half register its significance as you look back to check, then look away again prior to the full realization and reaction – in other words, you simply add an extra head turn. Again, this will only work if you can make this more convoluted physicality look truthful in terms of your thought processes. Indeed, it is theoretically possible to do triple and quadruple 'takes' provided you can back them up with appropriate reality of thought. It might be interesting for you to see how many head turns you can make before the final reaction. However, make sure that you can think fast enough, otherwise you will look as if you are just maniacally jerking your head.

Taking the 'Take' Further

This format can be applied in many other comic situations and scenes, and can be developed further. It can also be used with dialogue in much the same way as before. Examine the following short scene. Some stage directions are in brackets and the manner in which the 'take' works should be clear:

(*A approaches B in the street. A is self-absorbed in thought. B is dressed as a bright pink banana.*)

A: Hello B.

B: Hello A.

The end of another 'take'.

A: I like that pink banana suit you're wearing. (*Walking on.*)

B: Thank you.

A: (*Turning back in realization.*) A PINK BANANA SUIT!

Although the 'take' would seem to be most applicable to simple comic scenes like this or the Ghost Gag, it also appears frequently within the text of more sophisticated comedy plays. Consider the following dialogue between a female and male actor (**A** and **B** respectively), in which there is a need for the male actor to utilize the thought process of a 'take' in order to make one of his lines work properly. Once again, there are some stage directions in brackets.

A: (*Sidling up to **B** on a sofa.*) B, I've got something important to tell you.

B: (*Engrossed in a magazine he is reading.*) Oh yes.

A: Yes, it's something quite important.

B: (*Still only half engaged in the conversation.*) Oh yes.

A: In fact, it's very important.

B: Oh yes.

A: Very important indeed.

B. (*Still reading.*) What's that then?

A: I'm pregnant.

B: That's nice for you ... (*Suddenly realizing what has been said.*) Did you say pregnant?

This scene does not require the same physicality of the 'take' that was apparent before, as **A** remains looking at his book until his final exclaimed question. However, apart from this, the principle is exactly the same. It is also interesting to note that the words 'Oh yes' are repeated three times. The 'Rule of Three', coupled with the actor intoning the words in exactly the same way each time, will create a natural rhythm and progression towards the climax of the scene; it is perfectly natural and truthful to do this as **B** is not really concentrating or fully aware of what he is actually saying.

TIMING

It is reasonably obvious that proper execution of the 'take' and 'double take', in whatever form they may appear, requires an actor to be good at the one thing that is talked about most when referring to comedy – timing. Proper timing is essential in practically all areas of comic acting (and in some ways in other forms of acting too), and it is the ability to deliver lines with proper timing that marks out a good comedy actor. However, despite its importance, it is not especially easy to describe exactly what timing is and even less easy to teach an actor to be good at it.

In theory, timing is about the way an actor structures a text and how they employ pace and pause to get the best possible delivery of the comedy. In practice, it is largely a matter of 'feel' and instinct on the part of an actor: good comic timing cannot really be taught. However, everybody has natural timing of some sort (for it is used in everyday life) and it is certainly possible to analyse the technique that will allow you to make the best approach possible to the subject of timing in comedy. Begin this process by looking at another short, pantomime-like scene. It contains simple elements of comic timing, but requires a different kind of thought process to that of the 'take'. In this instance, the bracketed stage direction of 'pause' indicates the point at which good timing is required:

A: I have always wondered why you decided to settle in this godforsaken town.

B: I came here to forget.

A: To forget what?

B: (*Pause*) I can't remember!

The joke in this scene needs the pause to be just right. As usual, this is mainly achieved by using a correct and truthful thought process; this time, instead of being preoccupied, the actor is fully engaged in the conversation and must really reflect upon the question ('To forget what?') before answering it. If you try this you will see that timing, as with many other elements of acting, boils down to being able to back up the written word with natural thinking. It is the audience's subconscious recognition of this truthful approach that makes your timing work for them.

There are other, more technical, aids to making the timing of this particular joke work well. Try saying line two very dramatically and then, after duly considering the question, throw the final line away quite casually. Also, a longish inward breath as you pause, followed by a quick exhalation on the last line, will give a physical impetus that will automatically help with the timing. In this, you will be using your important 'Technical Brain' in order to obtain a truthful effect, but do not forget to use your equally important 'Truth Brain' in order to process these technical tricks in a real and natural way. There is nothing wrong with technical trickery provided it leads to truth and not falsehood in your acting.

Now examine another scene that approaches the issue of timing from a different angle but embodies exactly the same principles. This is a longer scene and the timing is far more varied and complex. There are no pauses

111

An expressive use of pause.

marked this time, in order to allow you to find your own organic timing through the scene. Experiment with pace and pause, but do so by finding the changes in speed and content of thought with each character in turn. Keep listening and thinking all the time and let the words find a pattern of their own. This scene is not particularly funny on the page, but timed well it can be extremely entertaining as the audience watches B try to extricate himself or herself from a predicament:

(*A has just returned from holiday. He visits* ***B*** *on his way home to pick up his car that* ***B*** *has been looking after for him in his absence. Unbeknown to him,* ***B*** *has taken the car out and crashed it.*)

A: Hello, B.

B: Hello, A. Did you have a nice holiday?

A: Wonderful, thank you. I've just popped in to pick up my car.

B: Sorry?

A: My car. I've come to get it.

B: Your car?

A: Yes. You've been looking after it for me.

B: Oh, that car.

'I just popped in to pick up my car.'

QUICK START GUIDE TO ACTING

17. Considering Comedy

When acting in comedy, there are several points to consider, in particular:

1. You must be real – good comedy is almost always based upon truth.
2. Your performance will often be required to be 'large' and of 'high energy' (although not always). Do not be afraid of this – if the script is good, you will still be able to remain truthful even though you will be pushing the threshold of reality hard.
3. On a purely technical level, don't forget to be ready for the audience to laugh and remember to wait for them. In order to do this, and to remain natural, you will have to 'hold' the last thought or allow the next to begin to formulate. Do not wait too long – 'ride' into the next line just as the laughter subsides. Acknowledge the audience's energy and work with it rather than against it.
4. Take every opportunity you can to work with both scripted and improvised comedy material: this is the only way that you will develop instinctive timing. However, remember that timing must be incorporated into your general technique, so that the audience is aware of your reality within the scene and not your desire to 'get laughs'. Never try to be funny – just play the truth of the comedy.

A: Yes.

B: The car I've been looking after for you.

A: Yes. It is here isn't it?

B: What?

A: My car.

B: Oh, your car's here, yes. Your car's here. It's definitely here. Oh, yes.

A: I see. It's in the garage is it?

B: Yes. That's right. It's in the garage. Or, at least, *a* garage.

A: What?

B: Good food was it ... at your hotel ... nice things to eat?

A: Yes, delicious. Now, can I have my car keys please?

B: Sandy beaches?

A: Pardon?

B: Were there sandy beaches ... at the resort?

A: I went to Paris.

B: Oh, yes. Silly me. What was it you wanted again?

A: My car!

B: And the food was good?

A: Yes. Now give me my keys before I lose my temper.

B: I had a nice holiday once. Nice food. Sandy beaches. Wasn't Paris ...

A: What have you done to my car?

B: Would you like a drink?

HEIGHTENED REALITY

To conclude this look at comedy technique, examine the following monologue and see if you can play it with a heightened degree of reality while still keeping it truthful. Allow your energy to be high and push the character as far towards caricature as you can, without losing the sense that this is a real person with genuine breath in their body and blood in their veins. It is from a children's play and, as children make the most demanding of audiences, it must be both funny and believable. Remember that good acting is not always about subtlety – it can be large, if necessary, as long as it is real.

(*Enter Sir Galahad, of King Arthur and the Knights of the Round Table fame. He is the complete antithesis of his brave and manly image, but he is very much the audience's friend and confidant. He calls the audience his 'Knights Auditoria' and here he addresses them directly.*)

Galahad: Long live King Arthur! Hello, you're the Knights Auditoria aren't you? I thought so. Sorry – it's just when you're at Round Table level you don't see much of the lesser Knights. Oh, sorry – that sounded snobbish, didn't it? I didn't mean it to come out like that. I'm always saying things I don't mean – it's a habit. I've got nothing to be snobbish about, anyway. I'm only on the Round Table because of me name – Sir Galahad. I'm supposed to be all gallant and sophisticated and good with women. Trouble is, I have a bit of a job living up to my legend. Actually I'm not like that at all. In fact, I'm a bit of an idiot really. I can't seem to get anything right. I put my armour on the wrong way round; when I swing my sword savagely round me head I fall off me horse; I tuck me tabard into me underpants. If I'm sent out to slay a horde of marauding invaders, I usually get the wrong ones. Last week I attacked the Second Camelot Scout Troop – well, they looked pretty vicious to me! I'm not very good at fighting at all really. You see, I'm not very brave. I'm supposed to be – but I'm not. Sometimes when we go into battle I shake so much the visor on me helmet rattles. Well it's not easy taking on these hard fighting, pillaging, barbarous, marauding, knight slayers ... some of them are quite rough, you know!

12 'THE PLAY'S THE THING'

PUTTING IT ALL TOGETHER

In this chapter you will have the opportunity to revise and consolidate all you have learnt by examining a fictitious play, and applying your techniques in all of the various areas of work that would be required were you to be actually rehearsing it for performance. The play is not presented as a full script but in the form of a synopsis and various character breakdowns and extracts for you to work on or think about in terms of the information you have studied in previous chapters. You must do this as if you were playing one of the six characters in the play. Choose the one that corresponds to your sex and is in the nearest age group to yours. The play is called *Entertaining Friends*. As you read the following information about the play and its plot, begin to formulate a feeling for what the play might mean to you.

SYNOPSIS

The play concerns two households in a fashionable and expensive suburb of London. It is not a comedy as such but, despite its serious subject matter, does have its lighter moments.

Karen and **Tim** are a couple in their thirties. They have lived together, reasonably happily, for ten years, but have always avoided the commitment of marriage and children – although this has been mainly been due to Karen rather than Tim. Their union has become something of a convenience to her,

taking second place to their respective highly successful careers and their upmarket lifestyle. Tim would like this to be different but enjoys the status quo.

Pat and **Neil** are near neighbours and members of the same tennis club. They are in their fifties and have been married for more years than they care to remember. Whilst they were blissfully happy once, their marriage has gone stale over time and has now become very much a pretence for the sake of respectability. They are a down-to-earth couple who have found themselves enjoying a high social status through their reasonable wealth earned from Neil's very successful haulage business.

Jane and **Peter** are Pat and Neil's children – both in their twenties. Peter works at the local supermarket as a shelf stacker and still lives at home. Jane is a doctor living and working in Scotland. Peter is unattached and something of a loner. Jane lives with an extremely successful surgeon who is also her boss.

The action of the play takes place on Boxing Day evening, in the house of Pat and Neil. Karen and Tim have been invited to dinner in order for Neil to ask Tim if he might be interested in a business proposition. The two couples have been good friends for some years, despite the age difference, but in recent months Neil has started a clandestine affair with Karen, of which their respective partners are, as yet, unaware. Jane is home for the Christmas holidays, having had a huge row with her partner before leaving. Both she and Peter are present for the dinner and, although

Peter is blissfully unaware of any problems at home, Jane has strong suspicions about her father's infidelity and views the evening as a hypocritical farce. In the course of the play the truth is revealed and all the characters' lives become irrevocably altered as a result.

The play is about love, betrayal and the barrenness of lives based upon material gain. However, it also examines the extraordinary tensions between family loyalty and the need for truth.

CHARACTERIZATION

For the exercise of examining this play in terms of character you will look at your chosen character and apply the methodology that you explored in Chapter 8. In order to promote and aid this process, look especially at the following character notes applicable to your character. These will summarize the basic character traits of each character and put them into the context of their importance within the play. They will also guide you towards the kind of physical and vocal characterization that you may be aiming towards. This gives you a starting point if you wish to work 'outside in' and a rough indication of where you might end up if working 'inside out'. However, these are only to be used as a framework – it is your intellectual character building that must lead to an honest physicality of each character in the play.

Do not ignore the other characters in the play, for it is part of your job to discover how your character has been affected and influenced by the others. Do not forget that you must embark upon a voyage of discovery

OPPOSITE: 'You're even more beautiful when you're angry.'

about these characters; you must not lose sight of your journey's end – finding a physical manifestation for them. This should, of course, include their postures, movements, voices and mannerisms, but you must also decide how they would be dressed during the course of the play.

Karen is a career woman. She is extremely ambitious, strong and apt to be a little hard and unemotional. She has begun to find Tim dull and conventional, and has embarked upon the affair with Neil more out of a need for excitement and change than any genuine feelings for him. Her manner is cool and brittle, and there is a great sense of defensiveness about the way she conducts herself: as if she were always afraid of exposing too much of her personality. Deep down, she is still in love with Tim but is beginning to realize that they have no future together anymore.

Tim is affable and relaxed. He too has enjoyed a successful career, but has not done so at the expense of losing his identity: he knows who he is and is happy in his own skin. He has a good sense of humour, an unshakable faith in human kind and a positive view of the future. He has always been grateful for the fact that Karen has taken a leading role in their lives and relationship and, in a sense, has become rather too dependent on her emotional resilience. He is genuinely unaware of Karen's disenchantment with their relationship and loves her devotedly.

Pat is very much a larger than life character: bossy and a little overbearing, but extremely good natured and kind nonetheless. She has not worked since marrying Neil, and has been a voracious homemaker and mother. She has enjoyed a luxurious lifestyle and a stable existence and, because of this, has tended to ignore her husband's 'wandering eye'. She is extremely proud of her daughter, but equally worried about the apparent aimlessness of her son. She has never been particularly intellectually intelligent, but has never really needed to be. Finding out about her husband's infidelity will not be the end of her world, but the ensuing break-up of her family will be.

Neil is a predator both in his business life and his dealings with the opposite sex. This is almost certainly not his first affair and his involvement with Karen is about bolstering his male ego and an attempt to ignore the fact that he is growing older. He is a self-made man and this has been achieved with an aggressive and forceful nature. However, he hides this beneath an exterior of charm and affability. He is constantly on the lookout to make more money.

Jane is serious and confident. She is ambitious professionally, but this has not detracted from her essential goodness and desire to help mankind and play a positive role in the world generally. She is intelligent and, more importantly, blessed with great common sense; she is extremely perceptive and very practical in her view of what she observes around her. Although she is good at giving advice to others she is not as good at taking it herself. She knows that her relationship with her boss, the surgeon, is based too much upon professional expediency and not enough upon love and commitment. Part of her reason for visiting this Christmas has been to make definite decisions about her future, but she has become distracted by the obvious problems at home.

Peter is hopelessly purposeless, lacking in any personal ambition and unaware of anything that is going on around him. He is quite happy in his own world and wants only to be left in peace to pursue his life in his happy but aimless state. He is not unintelligent but is extremely lacking in his sister's brand of common sense, and cannot understand why others seem to make life so complicated. He seems to exist in a constant state of low energy

and always prefers to drift along, waiting to see what life will bring to him next.

When you have worked on your character, make sure that you begin to allow their voice and physicality to materialize as you work on the extracts.

MONOLOGUES

In this section there are six extracts from the play, each of them a monologue spoken by each character. Read them all but concentrate upon your own. As you study it, pay particular attention to the following points:

1. Work out a 'map' of the speech (either in your head or on paper) of the basic thoughts and intentions behind the words.
2. Work out roughly where your energy bubbles will change and how.
3. Decide which thoughts are more important than others, with particular reference to those that might illuminate important themes of the play.
4. Be sure you know what your character knows about the overall situation and what they don't.
5. Decide what the technical requirements of the speech are (Technical Brain), and how you will apply them truthfully (Truth Brain).
6. Use your imagination to find a physical context for the speech – whether you are sitting or standing, still or moving, inactive or active (making coffee, washing-up, eating, drinking, smoking, and so on).

Karen: (*Alone with Neil in the kitchen.*) Tim has always been far too content with his lot. He lets his boss walk all over him; I know he does. He denies it, of course, but I can tell by some of the things he says that he gets treated like a doormat. That's what I like about you: you're your own man – you know what you want and you get it. Oh, Tim's done well; I admit that. But he could have done so much better: he could have really been someone. I'm sounding hard again, aren't I? What a bitch I must be to treat him like this. He doesn't deserve it, he really doesn't. He's just so infuriating sometimes. I came home from work the other day – he'd been taking some time off he was owed – and he'd laid on this romantic dinner: candles, what he thinks is my favourite song playing in the background, the lot. He was so pleased to see me home, so ... loving. And do you know, all I could think about was you. What made it worse was that I didn't feel guilty about it: I didn't care, I just didn't. And I don't care now. I'm not a very nice person, Neil, am I?

Neil: (*Alone in the living room with Tim.*) I've been meaning to have this little chat with you for a long time, Tim. I've got a scheme on the go that you might be interested in. Nothing too risky but very, very – what shall I say – potentially lucrative. A couple of contacts of mine are interested in opening a nightclub: an upmarket one – classy – something to cater for a more discerning clientele. They've asked me to come on board and, quite frankly, I've jumped at it. They know what they're about these fellows; they're bright as buttons, and going places. My business more or less runs itself these days. I've done very well, Tim, very well indeed. But now I need something to make life exciting again: something I can get my teeth into, if you know what I mean. Well, the bottom line is – there's room for another partner. We've raised most of the finance but another interested party

wouldn't go amiss, so I immediately thought of you – chance for you to get out of the rut – do something for yourself for a change, instead of lining the pockets of that company you work for. What do you think?

Jane: (*Alone in the dining room with Peter.*) I love Nigel; at least I think I do. No, of course I do. He's just not the right person for me to spend the rest of my life with. I thought he was at first, I really did. He was kind and attentive and made me feel special – all those things. I knew at the back of my mind that going with him would help my career but, at the time, I thought that was all right because I really did love him. But it wasn't all right – it was all wrong: I know that now. If I'm honest, I knew it then – I just didn't think about it. So now I need some time to think. I wasn't intending to come home this Christmas. Nigel wanted me to go up to meet his parents – they're highland aristocracy – lairds no less. And now I'm here I can't think about anything accept Mum and Dad, and what's happening to them. You really are stupid, you know, Peter – can't you see what's been going on all this time? No, of course you couldn't: you wouldn't spot a situation if it bit you on the leg. Mum is so trusting – at least she pretends to be. I'm not sure if she cares about what dad gets up to or not. She seems to be fine as long as we're all together. Meanwhile, Karen is getting everything her own way – well, not for much longer she won't.

Pat: (*In the dinning room with all seated for dinner.*) Right, well, I think that's everything. The greens look a bit anaemic but I didn't want to overcook them. Get started all of you; don't stand on ceremony, just help yourselves. I'm sorry

'Can't you see what's been going on all this time?'

there aren't any parsnips – I know how much you like them, Tim – but I forgot to pick them up when I did the big shop. This Christmas has been even more hectic than usual I'm afraid. We weren't expecting Jane – not that she isn't welcome – it's been a lovely surprise to see you, dear. Oh blast, I've forgotten to bring in the gravy – Peter, pop out and get it for me will you, there's a good boy. I shall be forgetting my own brain next. Neil, would you pass me the potatoes please. I hope you don't mind beef. I thought that cold turkey would be too much of a cop-out. Not that there isn't plenty of it left – Neil always buys too big a bird – we'll be eating it for most of next week I expect. Karen, what a lovely necklace you're wearing: I noticed it when you came in. It looks expensive. Did Tim give it to you for Christmas or have you got a secret admirer? Oh, by the way, has anybody met the new chairman's wife yet? She's got quite an eye for the men so I hear. You boys had better watch out. We don't want to lose our men, do we Karen?

Tim: (*Alone in the kitchen with Pat.*) Karen is doing very well at work, very well indeed. Another pay rise last month and I think they've got her in mind for the new branch when it opens. I'm extremely proud of her you know, Pat. I know she doesn't like me being so – she thinks it's patronizing, but I can't help it. She'd make a fantastic mother I think. Not that I dare mention it, I think she'd kill me: the career is all-important with Karen. It is for me, of course ... but maybe not as much. I'd have liked children really. I think we've left it a bit late now, but you never know. Lots of women have children in their forties now, don't they? So perhaps there's hope yet. We'll have to see what happens in the future. Neil's asked me to go in with him on this new nightclub venture of his – I expect you know. I'm very flattered, of course, but I'm not sure about it really. I mean, I know that Neil has checked it out – it's solid, I know that. It's just quite an investment. It could certainly change our lives; make us some money, I'm not denying that. But it's a big step – a very big step – well, for the likes of me anyway.

I'll have to talk it over with Karen when we get home. Where do these plates go?

Peter: (*With the others at the dinner table.*) I like it at the shop. I've got some good mates there. I'm happy. What's the point in earning goodness knows how much a year, with a company car and an expense account, if you hate every minute of it? At least I know who I am. I mean really know. I'm not too busy to even give myself the time of day. You see, it's all about freedom. Freedom from debt, freedom from worry, freedom from boring people who want to put you in a box all the time; who want you to perform like you're some kind of monkey at the circus. I don't owe anybody anything and nobody owes me. If I wanted to pack up tomorrow and take off, I could. No ties, you see, that's important. Don't get me wrong – I respect all you rat race people. I think you do a grand job and if that's what floats your boat, who am I to complain? It's just not for me, that's all – not my thing. I want to breathe the air when I want to; see the sky; taste life and not just sniff at it. Not exactly a chip off the old block, am I Dad?

DUOLOGUES

The next section contains three duologues, with each of the characters being in one of them. Be sure to read them all, not just the one that applies to you particularly. As well as working on the same six areas as suggested for the monologues, you should also consider the following extra points:

1. How might the way the other actor plays the scene affect your own interpretation and where are you most likely to receive strong impetuses from them?
2. As well as considering the bubbles of energy you are using when speaking, do

'I'd have liked children really.'

the same when you are listening: work out just how much of your attention is focused upon what is being said to you and how much upon your own thoughts.

3. Make sure that you are listening, looking and responding as naturally as possible and live 'in the moment' as completely as you can.

Peter: Dad and Karen. You are joking, aren't you?

Jane: Of course I'm not. It's not exactly a joking matter is it? I've had my suspicions for ages, and the looks they've been giving each other this evening just about confirms it.

Peter: But Dad wouldn't do that. Not to Mum.

Jane: Well, he is.

Peter: How long have you been nursing this fantasy?

Jane: Oh, it's been going on for a while I think. She's been wanting to get her claws into him ever since she first set eyes on him. Mind you, with a partner as wet as Tim, I'm not entirely surprised.

Peter: Tim's a good bloke.

Jane: Tim's a fool, and so are you if you can't see the blindingly obvious.

Peter: You're not going to make a fuss about this are you, Jane? If you've got it all wrong and you cause a big scene with Karen and Tim, I don't think Mum and Dad will be especially pleased.

Jane: I haven't 'got it all wrong', but no, I'm not going to do anything about it – not yet anyway.

Peter: Good. Just cool down a bit. It will all seem very different after Christmas, you'll see. Once you've got yourself sorted out with that Nigel bloke you'll feel better.

Jane: Are you suggesting that I'm projecting my own problems on to Mum and Dad, because if you are …

Peter: Shut up. They're coming back.

* * *

Karen: I suppose you find this evening highly amusing: all this 'happy families'?

Neil: You're even more beautiful when you're angry.

Karen: Does Pat know?

Neil: Of course she doesn't. At least, she hasn't said anything.

Karen: She's not stupid you know, Neil.

Neil: Well, Tim obviously is then. He seems completely unaware.

Karen: Tim is Tim.

Neil: He seems genuinely interested in my venture. That's all that concerns me.

Karen: You shouldn't have got him involved. You're asking for trouble.

Neil: Don't worry so much.

Karen: Where are we going with all this, Neil?

Neil: I wasn't aware that we were going anywhere. We are just having some fun, aren't we?

Karen: Is that all it is to you – a bit of fun?

Neil: Well, what do you want – to sail off into the sunset together, leaving our humdrum lives behind?

Karen: Be serious. I don't know what I want. Except, for some reason I just can't explain, I want you.

Neil: First sensible thing you've said all evening.

* * *

Tim: This is a lovely house you know, Pat. Really beautiful.

122

'I don't know what I want.'

Pat: Yes, we're very lucky.

Tim: More like hard work than luck I would say.

Pat: Well, it's Neil who has earned all the money. He's very good at being successful.

Tim: Yes he is.

Pat: And I am very good at being a successful man's wife – his faithful right-hand woman: no irony intended.

Tim: I sometimes feel that Karen and I are exactly the reverse.

Pat: Are you and Karen happy, Tim?

Tim: Yes, of course we are. Why shouldn't we be?

Pat: No reason. I just wondered. You've been together for quite a while.

Tim: Not as long as you and Neil.

Pat: No, that's true.

Tim: And you are both happy, aren't you?

Pat: Well, yes, I am.

Tim: Not Neil?

Pat: I'm not sure. I thought he was, but lately ...

Tim: What?

Pat: I sometimes think that it's only business that makes him truly happy.

Tim: Surely not?

Pat: Do you like these flowers? I do like to have flowers in the house in winter: they brighten everything up.

Tim: Yes, they're splendid.

Pat: Neil likes the house looking bright and cheerful. Would you help me take the coffee in?

IN CONCLUSION

If you can work on this fictitious play with others, so much the better. You should not only seek out a colleague to play the scenes with, but also others to act as the audience and give feedback upon your work. However you choose to approach the work, the main thing is to take enjoyment and pride in applying the techniques you have learnt in this book. Your next step must be to get out there and act as much as you can. If you remember the importance of your talent and technique, and you have enough integrity and belief in what you are doing to process this into truth on stage, then you will become a better actor every day.

FURTHER READING

RECOMMENDED FURTHER READING

All of the books by Stanislavski (published by Eye Methuen)

Barker, Clive, *Theatre Games* (Methuen, 1977)

Barkworth, Peter, *About Acting* (Secker & Warburg, 1980)

Berry, Cicely, *Voice and the Actor* (John Wiley & Sons, 1991)

Bicât, Tina and Baldwin, Chris (eds), *Devised and Collaborative Theatre* (Crowood, 2002)

Hartnoll, Phyllis, *The Theatre (A Concise History)* (Thames & Hudson, 1998)

Hodge, Alison (ed.), *Twentieth Century Actor Training* (Routledge, 1999)

Johnstone, Keith, *Improvisation and the Theatre* (Methuen, 1991)

Lloyd Evans, Gareth and Barbara, *Companion to Shakespeare* (J.M. Dent & Sons, 1990)

Perry, John, *The Rehearsal Handbook* (Crowood, 2001)

Potter, Nicole (ed.), *Movement for Actors* (Allworth Press, 2002)

Rodenburg, Patsy, *The Right to Speak* (Methuen, 1991)

Turner, Clifford, *Voice and Speech in the Theatre* (Malcolm Morrison, 2000)

INDEX

accent 72, 86
accept and build 45, 47, 51–52
acting:
  ability 65, 88
  aids 51
  commodity 81
  energy 95
  fundamentals 19
  in comedy 113
  properly 17–8, 36, 62
  servant 71
  technique 107, 109
  techniques 44, 97
  thoughts 28
action 21, 25
actions 18, 25, 29, 50, 91
age factor 58
agendas 57, 88
allow 85
amateur 9
analyse 13, 25, 89, 111
analysing 79
analysis 82
applause 14
appropriate noises 31
artistically 99
  appropriate 84
As You Like It 100
attack 29
audience 11, 13, 17, 23, 25, 41–2, 62, 65, 68–69, 80, 85, 89, 91, 93–5, 97, 99, 104, 108
auditorium 66, 95
authenticity 15
author 82
autopilot 40
awkward 17, 41, 63

bad actor 29
balancing 95
basic reactions 33
basics 11
'be' 15
belief 25, 124
believable 114
biography 84
blank (verse) 102
blueprint 18
body 53, 55–6, 58, 62–3, 65, 77, 87, 91–2
  image 55
  language 37
bomb 24
bottom line 11
breath 55, 66–71
breathing 13, 71, 55–6, 66–8
bubble 91–3, 95
  technique 91
bubbles 94–5, 97, 118
  of energy 89, 121

career 9
caricature 83, 86, 88, 107, 114
  caricature-like acting 87
Celia 103–5
centre 63
  centre of gravity 63
centred 62
centring 62
character 13–4, 17, 19, 23, 25, 31, 42–3, 48–51, 62, 77, 82–3, 85–7, 89, 91–3, 100, 109, 112, 114, 117–8
  actors 77
  breakdowns 115
  building 48, 117
  work 78, 81, 83
characteristics 82, 87
characterization 17, 53, 81, 83–4, 87, 117
characters 55, 65, 72, 75, 77, 80–2, 88, 100, 108, 117, 121
checklist 58
children 114
children's play 114
clarity 66, 72, 102
  clarity of action 108
  clarity of thought 22
class 83, 102
classical acting 29
classical actor 28
classless society 83
clearly plotted 99
collaborative effort 85
colour (of voice) 69
comedians 36
comedy 107–9, 111, 113, 115
  actor 111
  character 108
  plays 110
  sketch 36
  technique 107, 114
comfortable clothing 10, 55
comic acting 108, 111
comic concepts 107
comic timing 111
communal 36, 58
  activity 104
  spontaneity 38
communication 13–16, 18, 22, 29, 36, 53, 55, 66, 93, 100
  communication devices 18, 23, 33, 91
company 57, 82
Complete Works (of Shakespeare) 105
complexity 29, 99

computer 14
concentration 22, 40, 57, 58, 68, 86, 89, 91–7
consciously 58, 67
consonants 70, 73–4
constructive feedback 22
continuity of thought 29
control 58, 68, 70–1, 75
  energy 95
cooperative 33
  improvising 51
coordination 57–8, 77
costume 78
craft 9, 11, 58
craftsperson 15
cue 19
curtain 41

dame 108
dance 36, 58
dedication 11
deep breathing 67
definition of acting 11
delivering 97
delivery 11, 26
demonstrating 16–17, 22, 25
detail 102
develop 87, 97
developed 89
  developed and maintained 53
developing 81, 91
development 48, 51–2, 77
device 45, 81, 109
devising 45, 51
dialogue 21, 42, 95, 110
diaphragm 67–8
diction 72–3
director 39, 41, 43, 48, 50–1, 57, 82, 99
disciplined 29
double take (the) 109, 111
down to earth 21
drama 24, 53, 85, 100
drama schools 53
dramatic 47–9, 62
  communication 53
  effect 41
  theme 49
  themes 101
dramatically 29, 47, 72
dressing-up 87
duologue 33–4, 38, 121
dynamism 89, 91, 93–5, 97

emotion 13, 16–17, 25, 31, 41–2, 55, 92–4
emotional 62–3
  development 100
  energy 95
  memory 31

emotionally complex 77
emphasis 28, 39, 42, 51, 53, 69, 86, 101–2, 104
energy 55–6, 89, 91, 93–4, 96–7, 104, 113–4, 118
  level 29
entertaining 11
entrance 19
ethereal 97
ethnic background 83
exercise 10, 13, 15–7, 23, 28, 52, 55, 58, 79, 83, 86–8, 92, 95, 100, 102
exercises 58, 85
exhale 55
experience 9
experiment 13, 28–9, 49, 86–7, 91
experimented 39
experimenting 50–1, 109
expertise 53, 99
exploration 48, 50
exploring 83
  exploring text 51
express 14, 55
expression 22, 36–7, 53, 63
externally 77
eye contact 37
eyes 17

fabricating 15
face 28
facial expressions 22–3, 28, 37, 40
faithful servant 53
falling off the stage 19
falling over the furniture 19
false 16–7, 22
faster 39
fear 25
feedback 124
feel 25
feeling 102
feelings 16–8, 31
  of intention 27
female actor 100–1, 110
feminist 101
fictitious 14, 49, 62, 77, 83–4, 115
  play 124
finding the keys 24
fine-tuning 53, 65
first bubble 91–3
flexibility 52, 65, 77, 96
flexible 58, 68, 71, 91–2
fluidity 28
focus 25, 58, 91–5, 101–2, 108
following through 28
force 28

forcing 17
frustration 22
funny 114

gag 107
games 10
genius 99
gesture 15–7, 23, 28
gestures 22, 37, 40, 63
ghost 108–9
ghost gag (the) 107,
  109–10
glottal shock 72
gods 95
good acting 114
good actor 35, 77
grass roots 11, 21
groundwork 82
group 9, 16, 80, 86, 107
guide 25

hesitation 17
high drama 21
high energy 113
hobby 9
honesty 82, 87, 97
hot-seating 86–7
hum 68

iambic pentameter 102
idiosyncrasies 29, 75
illustrative 28
imagination 10–1, 15–6, 24,
  27, 48, 51–2, 56, 80, 82,
  84–6, 91, 93, 96, 118
imaginatively 47, 82, 85, 99
imperceptible 33
impetus 28, 103
improvisation 37, 41, 45,
  47–52, 78, 86–7
  comedy 113
  skills 52
impulses 17
in the moment 21, 121
inhibiting 67, 79
inhibition 52, 65, 69
input 41, 45, 52
inside out 81, 83, 87, 117
instinct 41, 111
instinctive 13–4, 22, 33, 39,
  45,87, 97
instructions 17
instrument 53, 55, 58, 65,
  77
integrity 15, 17, 19, 124
intensity 28
intentions 14, 18, 21–3, 29,
  31, 36–7, 55, 57, 85, 91,
  100–102, 104, 118
interact 21, 34
internalized 92–3
internally 77
interpersonal 57
interplay 33
interpret 13, 82, 92, 100
interpretation 17, 68, 92–3,
  97, 99, 100
interrogation scene 38
involuntary 16
isolation 28–9

jaw 68, 71–4
job 14–5, 23
journey 13, 81

keys 24
keyword 28
King Henry V 69

lack of spontaneity 15
language 101
laugh 107–9, 113
layering 29
lead actor 50
lead role 49
lifeless 37, 41
lifelike 14
lighting box 41
limber 58
  routine 58–9
  limbering 57–8
line 104
line of sight 41
lines 38, 48, 67, 111
lips 68, 70–3
listening 15, 17, 33, 37–8,
  40, 92, 112, 121
living in the moment 22,
  40
living the part 18, 21
looking 37, 109, 121
loose 57–8
louder 39

maintained 58, 77
maintenance 65
make-up 78
male actor 100, 110
male impersonation 103
mannerisms 117
map 25, 27–8, 36, 118
  of thought 27
  of thoughts 100
mapped 33
massage 58
meaning 101, 104
measured 28
mechanical 41
mental 95
  aid 56
  commands 27
  energy 89, 91–2
  focus 93
  processes 14, 77
mentally relaxed 56–8
metaphorical 89, 93
methodology 50, 117
mime 53
mind 14–5, 17–8, 25, 56,
  58, 91
mindset 15, 100
mobility 55
modern actor 101
modern playwright 103
moment-by-moment 34, 41
monologue 25, 29, 114,
  121
motivation 9, 41–3, 45, 88,
  94, 102
mouth 70–2, 74
move 57

movement 15, 22, 28, 36,
  53, 55, 57, 63, 67, 79,
  85, 87, 117
moving 18, 37
mugging 16
muscle 74
  memory 60
  movement 71
  tone 58

narrative 93
narrator 69
natural 13–6, 22, 40, 44, 55,
  66, 109, 111, 113
  impetus 23
  process of thinking 28
  repetition 25
  rhythm 111
  thinking 111
naturalism 23, 29, 33, 41,
  44, 100, 107
naturally 14, 17, 21–3, 25,
  57, 62, 71–2, 86, 121
navigating 19
neutral 72
new play 97
new thought device 29
normal progression 23
nose 71
not acting properly 19
note 70
notes 68, 101, 105

obediently 57
observer 21
observing 17, 40
of the moment 25
offstage 19
on stage 15, 19, 35, 45, 50,
  55, 57, 66, 87, 89, 91,
  97, 124
on text 37
onlookers 13, 15–6
open and free 15
openness 72
organic 11, 14, 40, 45, 112
  feedback 37
  technique 36
organically 18, 23, 39, 82,
  88
organs of articulation 73
outside in 82, 86, 117

pace 28–9, 41, 68, 86, 97,
  112
panic 23
pantomime 107–8, 111
  pantomimic comedy 109
paradoxically 104
parallel meaning 29
paraphrase 28, 93
park bench 51
part 38
part (the) 19
participant 51, 47, 109
particular thought 29
passionate 21
pattern of your thoughts 21
pause 41, 44, 111–2
pedestrian 21, 48, 103, 105

pen 21-3
penmanship 100
perfection 55
performance 16, 22, 55, 77,
  80, 95, 115
  skills 36
performer 35
performing 44, 57–8, 104
perseverance 97
persona 36
personal imagination 83
personality 23
Phebe 100, 103–5
philosophy 81
  of acting 81
phrase 69, 102, 104–5
phrases 29
physical 63, 77, 83, 95, 117
  activity 57
  attribute 83
  context 118
  fitness 58
  impetus 111
  manifestation 117
  qualities 87
  release 58
  requirement 109
  tension 55
  theatre 53
physicality 36, 62, 85,
  109–10, 117
physically 58
  blocked 57
  coordinated 62
  relaxed 58
physiology 67
physique 53
pitch 68, 70, 86
play 11, 14, 23, 36, 41, 45,
  48–50, 83, 93, 97, 115,
  117–8
played 104
playing 14, 25, 48–9, 66,
  75, 77, 81, 102
  comedy 107
  the part 18
  a scene 22
  a speech
  yourself 24
plays 99, 101
playwright 14, 22–3, 50, 83,
  85, 99, 100–1, 105
pliable 70
plot 115
poetic 99
political view 83–4
portray 36
posture 58, 117
potential 57
power 66, 68, 69–70, 89
practical 19
practice 85
practise 27
practised 53
practising actor 9
predetermined 21, 23, 39,
  51–2
  reactions 33
predictability 15
predictable 28

INDEX

prejudice 101
preordained 23, 34
preparation 28, 51, 55
preparatory work 29
prepared 15
pretence 14–15, 34
pretending 15, 22
pretentious 19, 51
priority 51
proactive 57
problem 14
process 56, 83–4, 94, 100
production 49
professional 9
project 66, 91, 93
projection 66, 89, 95
  of energy 66
prop 42
proper acting 10, 16–7,
  33–4, 39, 81
puppets 15
purpose 89

quality of voice 70

raw material 57
reactions 22, 24, 34, 50, 109
reading 28
real 97, 111, 113–4
  life 13, 22, 29, 48, 88
  time 33, 45
realism 15, 25, 31, 100
realistically 21, 25, 29, 49
reality 15, 19, 22, 41, 45,
  88, 103, 107–9, 113–4
  acting 19
  of the moment 42
received pronunciation 72
recreating reality 36
refocus 96
regime 58, 62
register 70
rehearsal 15, 18, 21, 35–6,
  41–2, 44–5, 51, 55,
  57–8, 85, 82, 96, 104,
  115
  period 49, 51, 87
  process 48
  room 51
relaxation 55, 58–9, 68,
  70–3, 77–8, 91
  exercise 55, 58
  of the mind 56
  techniques 58
relaxing 56–9, 71–2, 74
religious views 84
remedial action 65
remembering 28
  lines 19
rendition 37
resonance 79
resonant 67, 70, 73
resource 31
reversal 23
reversals 103
rhyming structure 102
rhythmic 104
ribcage 67
rigid format 27
roof (of mouth) 74

Rosalind 100–5
routine 58
rule of three 108, 111
rules 29
role 11, 48–9, 55, 77, 81,
  85, 97
replication 15, 22
response 21, 23, 33, 40,
  45, 48, 75, 121
rhythm 23, 56, 86, 102, 108

scenario 23–4, 51–2
scene 16, 18–9, 21, 23–5,
  29–31, 47–8, 50, 52, 66,
  94, 100, 108, 111–3,
  124
script 40, 43, 45, 48, 51, 85,
  113, 115
scripted comedy 113
scrutinizing 15
second bubble 93–4, 104
self-aware 81
self-doubt 65
sexual relationships 83
Shakespeare 68, 99–105
Shakespeare's men and
  women 102
Shakespearian 66, 72,
  100–1, 104–5
  actors 101
sham 34
Silvius 100
simulating 15
singers 36
skill 11
skills 10
slow breaths 55
small gestures 22
soliloquies 92
sound 65, 67–8, 70–2, 79,
  87
speaking 18, 28, 37, 66, 68,
  71–2, 74, 79, 86, 92,
  121
  lines 34
specific words 27
speech 25, 28–9, 36, 37, 63,
  72, 75, 92–6, 100, 102,
  104–5
speed 21, 28, 41, 112
  of thought 25, 28
spontaneity 15, 25, 33, 41,
  45
spontaneous 14, 22–3, 26,
  28, 51
  reaction 38
sport 57
stage 15, 23, 33, 35, 41, 53,
  88, 93, 95–6, 100
  presence 89, 95
stamina 58
starting point 27
state of mind 65
stilted 28
stimulation 25, 36, 38, 42,
  48, 109
strain 70
strength 77
stress 65, 70
stretch 59, 60–1, 73–4

stretched 58
strong 58, 93
structuring 51
students 15, 53
study of acting 9
subconscious 13, 33, 65, 67,
  91, 96, 111
subtext 29, 30
subtlety 87, 114
supple 58, 62
supporting character 49
suspended reality 34, 42
suspension of disbelief 14
synopsis 115

take 109–11
talent 9, 33, 57, 89, 124
teaching 9
technical 111
  ability 36
  brain 41–3, 107, 111, 118
  control 35
  demands 41
  directions 41
  exercise 81
  expertise 94
  level 113
  necessity 41
  problems 41
  requirement 39, 41–2,
    118
  trickery 111
technically 43–4, 70, 97
  demanding 19
  in command 35
technician 41
technique 9–10, 15, 19, 29,
  33, 36, 81–3, 89, 94,
  96–7, 100–11, 113, 115,
  124
tension 25, 55, 59–61, 67,
  70
text 10, 21, 26–9, 36–7, 41,
  45, 48, 50, 71, 83, 85,
  89, 92, 94, 99–103, 105,
  111
theatre 53, 95
theatrical 11, 45
  discipline 53
theme 49, 101. 118
theoretical 84
theory 85
thinking 25, 27, 29, 86, 109,
  112
  through 22
third bubble 94–5
thought 14, 16–8, 21–3,25,
  27–31, 36–7, 39, 45, 57,
  66, 89, 91–4, 100,
  102–4, 109, 112, 118,
  121
  patterns 22, 105
  process 110–1
  processes 26, 43, 100,
    109
thriller 42
throat 67–8, 70–1
timing 111–3
tone 86
toned 57–8

tongue 70–1, 74
  tip 74
tool 55
torso 67, 71
training 28
trigger 29
true acting 36
trust 18
truth 13–15, 17, 19, 21–23,
  25, 31, 36, 39, 41, 43–5,
  48, 77, 80, 82–3, 85, 88,
  92, 94, 97, 100–1,
  107–9, 111, 113–4, 118,
  124
  brain 41–4, 107, 111, 118
  instincts 41
  reaction 36
tuned 58, 75
tuning 53
two-brain theory 41, 44,
  107

uncoordinated 63
understanding 43
unnatural 15, 29
unnaturally 41
unreal 37
unreality 41
unrehearsed 45
unresponsive 57
upside down 23

variations 39
variety 22
verse form 102
verses 72
video 79
visual impetus 104
visual stimulus 25
vocal 62, 66, 70–1, 78, 117
  instrument 71
  projection 41
  skills 66
  technique 75
voice 14, 18, 23, 42, 53, 55,
  58, 65–6, 68, 70–1, 75,
  77, 79, 86–7, 95, 117
  work 65
volume 66–8, 70, 95
vowel sounds 70, 73
vulgarity 103
vulnerable 35
volunteer 13, 15–6

watch 33
watchable 94
way of thinking 19
weight placement 63
well prepared 19
wooden 15, 41, 87
word for word 28
words 25, 28–31
wordsmith 100
work 58
work-out 73
writer 99
written drama 45
written portrait 84